Tacitus Annals IV

The following titles are available from Bloomsbury for the OCR specifications in Latin and Greek for examinations from June 2021 to June 2023

Catullus: A Selection of Poems, with introduction, commentary notes and vocabulary by John Godwin

Cicero *Pro Cluentio*: A Selection, with introduction, commentary notes and vocabulary by Matthew Barr

Livy *History of Rome* I: A Selection, with introduction, commentary notes and vocabulary by John Storey

Ovid *Heroides*: A Selection, with introduction, commentary notes and vocabulary by Christina Tsaknaki

Tacitus *Annals* IV: A Selection, with introduction, commentary notes and vocabulary by Robert Cromarty

Virgil *Aeneid* XII: A Selection, with introduction, commentary notes and vocabulary by James Burbidge

OCR Anthology for Classical Greek AS and A Level, covering the prescribed texts by Aristophanes, Homer, Plato, Plutarch, Sophocles and Thucydides, with introduction, commentary notes and vocabulary by Simon Allcock, Sam Baddeley, John Claughton, Alastair Harden, Sarah Harden, Carl Hope and Jo Lashley

Supplementary resources for these volumes can be found at
www.bloomsbury.com/OCR-editions–2021–2023
Please type the URL into your web browser and follow the instructions to access the Companion Website. If you experience any problems, please contact Bloomsbury at academicwebsite@bloomsbury.com

Tacitus *Annals* IV:
A Selection

Chapters 1–4, 7–12, 39–41, 52–54, 57–60, 67–71, 74–75

With introduction, commentary notes and
vocabulary by Robert Cromarty

BLOOMSBURY ACADEMIC
LONDON · NEW YORK · OXFORD · NEW DELHI · SYDNEY

BLOOMSBURY ACADEMIC
Bloomsbury Publishing Plc
50 Bedford Square, London, WC1B 3DP, UK
1385 Broadway, New York, NY 10018, USA

BLOOMSBURY, BLOOMSBURY ACADEMIC and the Diana logo
are trademarks of Bloomsbury Publishing Plc

First published in Great Britain 2020

Cover design: Terry Woodley
Cover image © PjrTravel/Alamy Stock Photo

A catalogue record for this book is available from the British Library.

A catalog record for this book is available from the Library of Congress.

ISBN: PB: 978-1-3500-6030-2
         ePDF: 978-1-3500-6032-6
         eBook: 978-1-3500-6031-9

Typeset by RefineCatch Limited, Bungay, Suffolk
Printed and bound in India

To find out more about our authors and books visit www.bloomsbury.com
and sign up for our newsletters.

Contents

Preface

The text and notes found in this volume are designed to guide any student who has mastered Latin up to GCSE level and wishes to read a selection of Tacitus' text of the *Annals* in the original.

The edition is, however, particularly designed to support students who are reading Tacitus' text in preparation for OCR's AS/A-level Latin examination June 2021–June 2023. (Please note this edition uses AS to refer indiscriminately to AS and the first year of A level, i.e. Group 1.)

The text focuses on the rise to prominence of the Praetorian Prefect, Lucius Aelius Sejanus, and his attempts to manoeuvre himself into a position whereby he may have succeeded to the Principate. The period is one rife with political intrigue and faction, where one is always forced to question the motives and actions of the key figures.

This edition contains a detailed introduction to the context of the *Annals*, supported by a family tree and references to other original sources on the events. The notes to the text itself aim to help students bridge the gap between GCSE and AS level Latin, and focus therefore on the harder points of grammar and the style of the author. At the end of the book is a full vocabulary list for all the words contained in the prescribed sections, with words in OCR's Defined Vocabulary List for AS Level Latin flagged by means of an asterisk.

Rob Cromarty
June 2019

Introduction

Tacitus and history

...quod praecipuum munus annalium reor ne virtutes sileantur utque pravis dictis factisque ex posteritate et infamia metus sit.

...this I deem to be the principal responsibility of history, to prevent virtues from being silenced and so that crooked words and deeds should be attended by the dread of posterity and infamy.

Tacitus, Annals III.65.1

This remark encapsulates much of Tacitus' attitude towards annalistic history, reflecting his moralistic tendencies. For Tacitus, history had an inherently didactic purpose, to encourage Roman behaviours and safeguard the key qualities that he himself valued: freedom of speech, republican sentiments and the primacy of the Senate as the chief legislative body.

Thus his history is necessarily subjective, greatly influenced by his own attitudes and experiences. For example, he is particularly dismissive of the opinions of the urban plebs, claiming that they are simply 'desirous of pleasures, and delighted if a princeps inclines in the same direction' (*Ann.* XIV.14.2). Therefore, a key issue in reading Tacitus is to understand how his own historical context affected his interpretation of history.

Cornelius Tacitus' life is frustratingly vague for us, with our information coming primarily from inferences from his own works and references in the letters of the Younger Pliny. We may infer that Tacitus was born an *eques*, as the form of his name suggests, around AD 55: Pliny (*Epistles* VII.20.3–4) indicates that Tacitus was a few years older than Pliny himself, who was born in AD 61/2. Tacitus was also not of Roman stock, as we may infer from the remark *Italicus es an provincialis?* (Pliny, *Ep.* IX.23). He began his public career under Vespasian, and may well have been adlected to the Senate by that emperor; subsequently being advanced by Titus and Domitian. We know that in AD 88 he was a praetor (*Ann.* XI.11), although the precise details of his early career are uncertain. However, we do know that in AD 77 he was betrothed to the daughter of the celebrated general Gnaeus Julius Agricola (*Agricola* 9), with the marriage itself taking place in AD 78. It was most likely Domitian's ill treatment of Agricola, and that same emperor's abuse of the Senate as a whole which embittered Tacitus and ultimately coloured his interpretations of the reigns of the earlier emperors. Indeed the *Agricola*, his biography of his father-in-law, would suggest that he witnessed some of the atrocities of Domitian (*Agr.* 45), most likely in the period AD 93–96, where Cassius Dio (LXVII.12.1–14.4) gives details of the various executions and expulsion of leading citizens that he perpetrated.

During the reign of Nerva, Tacitus was appointed as suffect consul in AD 97, and in the years that followed there are several anecdotal references to his counsel and eloquence in various environs, including the law courts (e.g. Pliny, *Ep.* II.11). Tacitus was certainly proconsul of Asia in AD 113, but beyond this little is known of his final years, though we surmise from circumstantial evidence (such as his descriptions of the eastern boundary of the empire in *Ann.* II.61) that he lived until the end of AD 117, most likely dying shortly thereafter.

While Tacitus makes claims for his impartiality as an historian (*Ann.* I.1) because he lived after the events that he describes, a writer who is not a contemporary may have passions and prejudices equally as much as those who are. For Tacitus, it was the crimes and attitudes that he witnessed under Domitian that led him to see the possibility for abuse that the Principate afforded: in particular the treatment of Agricola – whose death in AD 93 he believed to have been caused or hastened by emissaries from the emperor – must have affected Tacitus deeply. The *Agricola* leads us to see that Domitian's envy of Agricola for his military successes in Britain, coupled with his own jealous possession of power, entailed that he could brook no rival. Thus power is abused in order to preserve control of that same power.

It is the beginnings of this tyranny that Tacitus perceived in the reigns of the earlier emperors, particularly that of Tiberius, with his enforcement of the law of treason (*Ann.* I.72.2) which gave rise to the swathe of *maiestas* trials (essentially treason trials) that dominate Tacitus' account of the period. These cases, almost universally directed against leading equestrians and senators, were symptomatic of the worst of the Principate – the suppression of freedom, the intolerance of political debate, and the jealous guarding of the burgeoning autocracy of the Princeps, which Augustus had strived so hard to disguise during his own reign.

However, Tacitus' obvious bias has led to criticism, and his presentation must never be taken at face value. While Tacitus' facts are rarely incorrect, his interpretation of them is frequently open to scrutiny. His account of the reign of Tiberius in *Annals* I–VI is no longer accepted as being wholly representative of the period; Tacitus' eye is too cynical and his moral stance is too monotone, one may easily see his villains as almost melodramatic in their villainy.

Yet despite this Tacitus does demonstrate some skills that are commendable as a historian. He professes a careful collation of previous sources (e.g. *Ann.* IV.10 and 57), indicating the use of a number of authorities through phrases such as *tradant plerique*. He equally knew the speeches of Tiberius (as one may observe in *Ann.* IV.8) and may have studied them in the *acta senatus*, as is suggested by his detailed reporting of senatorial procedure. However, the possibility remains that even in the case of the speeches, the original versions may have been adapted to better fit Tacitus' own interpretations. For in history, the figures may become characters in the hands of our authors. Here we may remember the observation of Thucydides that he:

... has put into each speaker's mouth sentiments proper to the
occasion, expressed as I thought he would be likely to express them.

Thucydides, *History of the Peloponnesian War* I.22

But equally Tacitus also reports traditional contemporary views and
rumour, although often openly acknowledging it as such. For example,
he recounts a version of the death of Drusus (Tiberius' son) that
inculcates Tiberius himself in the death (*Ann.* IV.10–11). While never
claiming it as fact – indeed he claims that in his recounting of it he
may 'banish false rumours by a clear example' (*ut claro sub exemplo
falsas auditiones depellerem*: *Ann.* IV.11) – his inclusion of it reinforces
his own opinions about the people involved. The seed is planted, the
contemporary negative perception of Tiberius is given prominence,
while Tacitus himself may be freed from direct accusations of
character assassination by virtue of his refusal to accept the rumour
that he discusses at length.

Indeed, Tacitus' bias against Tiberius and his reign has the merit of
being overt. Thus we as readers may account for this and argue against
it accordingly. The passion of his conviction is in some way admirable,
as he is writing purposefully to prevent both history and subsequent
emperors forgetting the offences and abuses of the past. It was this
purpose that led him to stress aspects of history to a degree which to
modern eyes seems far too subjective.

Yet in terms of the corruptive nature of power, in terms of the
issues of human weakness, and in terms of his adherence to his own
moral truth, Tacitus is an admirable author and a skilled student of
human nature.

The beginnings of Tiberius' reign

Crucial to understanding and accounting for the rise of Sejanus are
the events at the outset of Tiberius' reign.

At the death of Augustus there was no precedent for Tiberius to follow. Although Augustus had made him his heir, had finally given him proconsular imperium equal to his own, and had clearly groomed him in the public eye as his successor, he could do no more than that. When he died, the *auctoritas*, the supreme authority by virtue of which he was princeps, which he had acquired through his long pre-eminence and particular personality, died with him. It was this that Tiberius lacked.

Tiberius' position was in many ways a very strong one. His power was far greater than that of anyone else in the state, he had command of the armies (by virtue of his proconsular imperium) and he had no serious rivals. As Augustus' personal heir he was in possession of his vast fortune with all the power of patronage which that afforded him. Also, Augustus had been in power for a very long time and peace and stability had become generally established.

Nevertheless, Tiberius' position was also very delicate. He had to exercise power immediately, and be seen to be doing so, vis-à-vis the people and the army, while at the same time appearing to the Senate as not wishing to do so, and waiting for them to confer upon him the authority to do what he had already done. By trying not to offend the susceptibilities of the Senate, he laid himself open to a charge of blatant hypocrisy.

Let us first examine what actually happened, which is difficult given that the various authors offer different versions of the events. For instance, details of Augustus' very last day vary. Tacitus says, 'It is unknown whether he [Tiberius] found Augustus alive or dead' (*Annals* I.5), whereas Suetonius twice asserts that Augustus and Tiberius had a long 'confidential talk' together before the former's death (*Augustus* 98; *Tiberius* 21). Tacitus' slight at Livia – 'Some suspected his wife of foul play' – is too commonplace a rumour to be taken seriously. Suetonius' version of the loving partner of fifty-two years, who was at his bedside when he died, is more reasonable. 'Then', says Tacitus, 'two pieces of news became known simultaneously. Augustus was dead and Tiberius was in control'.

'The new reign's first crime was the assassination of Agrippa Postumus' (Augustus' grandson; *Annals* I.6). So begins Tacitus' version of Tiberius' Principate. It is uncertain whether he was killed on the orders of Augustus, Livia or Tiberius, as the sources show. The last seems the most unlikely, as Tiberius would hardly have considered referring the matter to the Senate had he been responsible. But, because the facts were never disclosed, suspicion inevitably rested on Tiberius. Why was Agrippa Postumus' death considered necessary? He had originally been banished under military guard for *ferocia*, and disinherited publicly in the Senate by Augustus, but his crime was probably political, as in the case of the two Julias, his mother and sister. He was the last direct male heir on the Julian side of the family, and the last throw for the political group which had centred on the elder Julia. Thus his very existence must have seemed a possible threat to the smooth transition of the Principate to the Claudian Tiberius.

It is clear that on Augustus' death Tiberius immediately took control. He assumed command over the Praetorian Guard, sent despatches to the army and provided himself with a bodyguard: 'He sent letters to the army as though he were already emperor' (Tacitus *Annals* I.7). True. He had to. No one else had the authority to do so, and it was crucial that there should be no hiatus in control over the armies. As it was, the very fact of Augustus' death sparked off mutinies in Pannonia and Lower Germany.

In the following days Tiberius accompanied Augustus' body back to Rome. There he convened the Senate by means of his *tribunicia potestas*, but only to discuss the funeral arrangements for Augustus. The oath of allegiance was also sworn to him, first by the consuls, the commander of the Guard and the controller of the corn supply, then by the Senate, army and people.

So far, so good. But Tiberius' position was still in limbo. On 17 September the Senate met again. It is difficult to know exactly what Tiberius was offered at this meeting, what he rejected, and whether the debate (or farce, as Tacitus calls it) continued into other sessions. What is clear is that Tiberius would not accept what he was offered straight away. What was it that Tiberius wanted? What was he trying to get the Senate to do? No doubt he wanted the Senate freely and willingly to accept him as their princeps (But how, as Tacitus might say, could the Senate act freely when Tiberius had all the power and they had no choice?). He also, probably quite genuinely, wanted to hold power in a less autocratic way than had Augustus, for with his patrician background he respected the traditions of the Senate. He also knew what a 'monstrous beast the monarchy was' (Suetonius *Tiberius* 24), 'what hard hazardous work it was' (Tacitus *Annals* I.11), and may seriously have wished to devise some way of sharing the load.

It appears that Tiberius failed in what he was trying to achieve. The more he declared himself unfit for the task, the more the senators clamoured for him to undertake it. Indeed, it must be pointed out that if Tiberius was acting without precedent, so was the Senate. They did not know what they had to do to legitimize him as princeps and they could have been genuinely in the dark as to what he was about. His language tended to be obscure at the best of times, and in such a discussion as this he could not say clearly what he wanted. It is possible that the Senate could not understand his suggestions; it is also possible that they would not.

Of the members of the Senate, many would have been Tiberius' own supporters, or supporters of Augustus, who would dutifully follow his successor. Some were new men brought in by Augustus and had only served under a princeps. To his personal followers it would be advantageous to have Tiberius as the new princeps, whereas to the new men it did not matter who was, as long as somebody was. Even those hostile or indifferent to Tiberius would see quite clearly that nobody else had any authority over the armies. With two armies in a state of mutiny, one of which was supposedly inciting Germanicus to bid for power, there may well have been fear and panic at Rome. Even senators could be forgiven for grovelling at the feet of Tiberius if they were doing it not from flattery, but to avoid civil war. Likewise Tiberius' suggestion that power might be shared could have been received with horror. In Rome's past, times of power-sharing – the triumvirates – had been bloody and terrifying. Those ambitious enough to have wished to take part in any such scheme would not have been allowed to do so by the rest.

Finally Tiberius had to acquiesce in a situation from which he could not escape. In order to continue the Principate at all, which was essential for the well-being of the empire, he had to act in ways he did not wish to. The autocracy of the system, which he plainly saw, he could not change; the help he needed he could not have. He was to try to achieve by his actions what he could not achieve formally, but in the end the inherent contradictions in the Principate were too much for him. It was this dichotomous situation that allowed for the rise of the ultimate political opportunist: Sejanus.

Annals Book IV

Book IV covers the years AD 23–28, which are typically seen as pivotal in Tiberius' reign, including such events as the death of Drusus, a series of maiestas trials, and the emperor's voluntary withdrawal to Capri in AD 26. It is therefore a period of major political upheaval, one which Tacitus presents as being paralleled by a complementary degree of moral inversion. Indeed, later in the *Annals*, Tacitus will describe Tiberius as a victim of the corrupting effects of autocratic authority:

In spite of all his experience of public affairs, Tiberius was transformed and deranged by absolute power.

Ann. VI. 48

When the Emperor is a bad man, and rules badly, misery ensues. Oppressive rule causes – and is caused by – moral degeneracy.

The opening section of our Book reinforces the sudden shifts and twists in morality and politics that will dominate its content:

> *... nonus Tiberio annus erat compositae rei publicae, florentis domus ... cum repente turbare fortuna coepit ...*

> ... the ninth year for Tiberius was of a peaceful republic and a flourishing household ... when fortune suddenly began to be disruptive ...

Ann. IV.1.1

The reason for this sudden reversal of fortune is the key figure of Book IV: Lucius Aelius Sejanus.

Lucius Aelius Sejanus hailed from Volsinii in Etruria. He and his father shared the Praetorian Prefecture until AD 15 when his father, L. Seius Strabo, was promoted to be Prefect of Egypt, a position which was very much the pinnacle of an equestrian career under the Principate. Sejanus, as sole Prefect of the Guard, enjoyed powerful connections to senatorial houses and had been a companion to Gaius Caesar on his mission to the East in 1 BC–AD 4. Through a combination of energetic efficiency, fawning sycophancy and outward displays of loyalty, he gained the position of Tiberius' closest friend and advisor. One development that favoured Sejanus was the concentration of all nine cohorts of Praetorian Guardsmen into a single camp at Rome. Augustus had billeted these troops discretely in small towns around Rome, but now Tiberius – undoubtedly with Sejanus' encouragement, perhaps even at his suggestion – brought them into the city, probably in AD 17 or 18. Sejanus, therefore, commanded some 9,000 troops within the city limits. As Sejanus' public profile became more and more pronounced, his statues were erected in public places, and Tiberius openly praised him as 'the partner of my labours'. Indeed, a good example of Sejanus' overt loyalty to Tiberius is the incident in Spelunca (Sperlonga) in AD 26, on which see Tac. *Ann.* IV.59 (Suet. *Tib.* 39 makes no mention of Sejanus' role in the incident). But Sejanus had ambitions far beyond even this.

According to Tacitus, Sejanus' first subversive act was the seduction of Tiberius' daughter-in-law, Livilla, who was at the time married to Drusus (II), Tiberius' son. Drusus (II), it would appear, resented Sejanus' influence over his father so the Prefect, in conjunction with Livilla, poisoned him in AD 23 (Tac. *Ann.* IV.3–8; Suet. *Tib.* 39; Dio LVII.22.1). It remains suspicious that no inkling of foul play in Drusus' death was entertained until eight years later, when Sejanus' ex-wife, Apicata, 'revealed' the matter in her suicide note. Quite possibly, Drusus died of natural causes and Sejanus' involvement is merely speculative. There followed a series of attacks on Agrippina's friends, mostly played out in the courts in the guise of charges of treason (maiestas) but, in Tacitus' account, actually the work of Sejanus, such as those against C. Silius and Sosia Galla in AD 24 (Tac. *Ann.* IV.18–20), Claudia Pulchra in AD 26 (Tac. *Ann.* IV.52) and T. Sabinus in AD 28 (Tac. *Ann.* IV.68–70; Dio LVIII.1.1b–3). There is some doubt, however, as to how many of the cases Tacitus ascribes to him were actually the work of Sejanus, see Levick, *Tib. the Pol.*, 163–4.

Then, in AD 25, Sejanus asked Tiberius for permission to marry Livilla, Drusus' widow, a request which Tiberius refused. This setback for Sejanus was somewhat mitigated in the following year, when the ageing emperor withdrew from Rome to live on Capri; he was never to return to the city. Tiberius was encouraged in his decision to retire by Sejanus, who now became the chief vehicle of access to the emperor. With Tiberius absent, Sejanus vented his full fury against Agrippina's family, whose demise he had been plotting for some time. In rapid succession Agrippina and her eldest son, Nero Caesar, and eventually also Drusus (III) Caesar, who had been involved in his brother's downfall, were arrested, convicted and imprisoned. By AD 31 Sejanus had reached the pinnacle of his power and was seen very much as the de facto emperor himself. The sources paint a picture of senators lining up to pay respects to a man they considered their social inferior (see Dio LVIII.5.1; LVIII.2.7–8).

What exactly Sejanus was aiming at remains a matter of debate. The Prefect's attacks against Agrippina and his proposal to marry Drusus' (II) widow, Livilla, suggest that he was attempting to follow the precedent of Agrippa. That is to say, an outsider who became the emperor's successor through a combination of overt loyalty, necessity and a family alliance forged by marriage. Tiberius, perhaps sensitive to this ambition (see *Ann.* IV. 40.4–40.7), rejected Sejanus' initial proposal to marry Livilla in AD 25, but later put it about that he had withdrawn his objections with the result that in AD 30 Sejanus was betrothed to Livilla's daughter (Tiberius' granddaughter). The Prefect's family connection to the imperial house was now imminent. In AD 31 Sejanus held the consulship with the emperor as his colleague, an honour Tiberius reserved only for heirs to the throne. Further, when Sejanus surrendered the consulship early in the year, he was granted a share of the emperor's proconsular power. When he was summoned to a meeting of the Senate on 18 October in that year he probably expected to receive a share of the tribunician power, the power that had been used since the inception of the Principate to designate would-be heirs, a development that would have seen the realization of all of his ambitions.

The ancient sources are vague on Sejanus' goals: Tacitus (*Ann.* IV.1, 3) merely states that he wanted *regnum*; Dio (LVII.22.4b) says he aimed at power; Suetonius (*Tib.* 65.1) claims the Prefect was a revolutionary; and Josephus (*AJ* XVIII.181) comments that Sejanus led a conspiracy, but omits mention of its purpose. Modern opinion is divided. Perhaps the best explanation for Sejanus' goals is that put forward by Levick (170–71), since taken up by Shotter (*Tiberius Caesar*, 42–4), that Sejanus aimed at being to Tiberius what Agrippa had been to Augustus: the trusted servant who would succeed to the throne. This explains Sejanus' attacks on Tiberius' successors (Drusus and the family of Germanicus) and is echoed in two comments in the sources: in Tacitus (*Ann.* IV.3) when he comments that a house full of Caesars was an obstacle to Sejanus' plans, and in Dio (LVII.22.4b) when he expressly says that Sejanus wanted to succeed Tiberius.

But in a shocking and unexpected turn of events, the letter sent by Tiberius from Capri initially praised Sejanus extensively, and then suddenly denounced him as a traitor and demanded his arrest. Chaos ensued. Senators long allied with Sejanus headed for the exits, the others were confused – unsurprising given this tumultuous about turn from Tiberius. The Praetorian Guard, the very troops formerly under Sejanus' command, but recently and secretly transferred to the command of Q. Sutorius Macro, arrested Sejanus, conveyed him to prison, and shortly afterwards summarily executed him. A 'witch-hunt' ensued, in the course of which Sejanus' family was arrested and executed; Livilla perished; followers and friends of Sejanus were denounced and imprisoned, or tried and executed; with some committing suicide in expectation of the verdicts. All around the city, grim scenes were played out, and as late as AD 33 a general massacre of all those still in custody took place (see Dio LVIII.5.5–11.5, the only surviving narrative account).

Tiberius himself later claimed that he turned on Sejanus because he had been alerted to Sejanus' plot against Germanicus' family. This explanation has been rejected by most ancient and modern authorities, since Sejanus' demise did nothing to alleviate that family's troubles: Agrippina remained under house arrest, Drusus was still housed in the Palatine's dungeons, and both died violently within three years of Sejanus' removal. Tiberius is also said to have discovered Sejanus' part in his own son's death in AD 23; the source of this information, however, is suspect. Possibly, in the highly charged atmosphere surrounding Sejanus' fall, the news acted as a catalyst, but its truth cannot be verified. Whatever the precise reasons, Sejanus' career and demise, and that of those around him, was an object lesson in the dangers of imperial politics. To achieve power under the emperors, the ambitious needed to get close to the source, but getting too close could lead to catastrophe, for both the aspirant and any who sought to feather their own nests by aligning themselves to said individual.

If for Tacitus Tiberius is the villain, then Sejanus is very much his right-hand man. It is difficult to convincingly describe the level of vitriol that Tacitus deploys against Sejanus, but he is blackened like no other character in the *Annals*. He is accused of being sexually perverse (*Ann.* IV.1.2), corrupt and power-hungry (*Ann.* IV.1.3), and able to manipulate Tiberius to a tremendous degree (*Ann.* IV.1.2). Sejanus is the prime example of the type of political opportunist who prospered under the Principate. When power rests in the hands of a single individual, it can easily be abused and usurped. That is what Sejanus sought to do.

As commander of the Praetorian Guard Sejanus had privileged access to Tiberius and quickly exploited this for his own ends, primarily that of engineering himself into the succession. Tiberius' credulity where Sejanus is concerned may be explained by the fact that, at the outset of his reign, he begged the Senate for colleagues to assist him (*Ann.* I.11.1; Suetonius, *Tiberius* 25). Finding no ready volunteers from within that body, it is unsurprising that he came to rely so heavily on Sejanus.

Velleius Paterculus, whose history was published before Sejanus' eventual downfall, is glowing about him (*History of Rome* II.127.1– 128.4), calling him a 'distinguished assistant', that he enjoyed a 'long-standing regard' from both people and emperor, and that he 'shared the burdens of the imperial office'. Here we see once again the sycophancy of the Senate towards the powerful. Dio (*Roman History*, LVIII.4.1) affirms this view, claiming that the senators and other sections of society treated Sejanus 'as if he were actually emperor', and that Tiberius called him the 'Sharer of my Cares'.

This leads naturally on to a brief treatment of the themes and motifs of Book IV, focussing as it does upon this relationship between Tiberius and Sejanus. Necessarily, these themes perhaps serve to elucidate more about Tacitus as a historian than they illuminate the figures whose actions he narrates. Those linked with the style of the writing will be treated in the next section, but here it would seem useful to treat the concepts of power and tyranny, as they play such a major role in the Tiberian hexad.

Tacitus' entire attitude to the power of the Principate is interesting, with a full treatment beyond the scope of this volume. While he benefitted from personal advancement under the Flavians, there seems to be a growing sense of guilt over his position in a Senate which was now largely 'toothless' in terms of its actual political authority. This perhaps accounts for the individuals whom he celebrates – Thrasea Paetus (*Ann.* XIV.12; XVI.21–35), Helvidius Priscus (*Hist.* IV.5–8), Domitius Corbulo (*Ann.* XI.18–20; XIII.8.2–9.3, 34.2–42.3; XV.1–17.3), to say nothing of his father-in-law Agricola – all evoke republican qualities, which Tacitus himself perhaps felt were no longer as visible in either himself or the majority of Rome's leading citizens. We should remember that Augustus had very much changed the political landscape of the empire, having 'enticed the soldiery with gifts, the people with food, and everyone with the sweetness of inactivity' (*Ann.* I.2.1). He notes that when Augustus died in August AD 14, and Tiberius navigated the acquisition of power in early September, that there was at Rome 'a headlong rush into servitude from consuls, fathers, equestrians' (*Ann.* I.7.1) and that, following Tiberius' speech on 17 September of that year, the Senate 'prostrat[ed] itself in the basest protestations' (*Ann.* I.12.1). Tacitus sums up the situation with his typical pithiness in his blunt question (*Ann.* I.3.7): 'what size was the remaining proportion [of Romans], who had seen the republic?'

If such was the situation when Augustus died, the demise of the republic and its morality – both key interests of Tacitus himself – was an even more distant memory by Tacitus' own lifetime. He notes that this malaise extended to historians too:

> At the same time [as the writing of history fell idle] truth was shattered under a variety of blows. Initially it was ignorance of politics, which were no longer a citizen's concern; later came the taste for flattery or, conversely, hatred of the ruling house. So between malice on one side and servility on the other the interests of posterity were neglected.
>
> *Histories* I

His summary of the Julio-Claudian period reveals much of his own concerns: a dislike for sycophancy; a hatred of censorship; the disenfranchisement of the citizenry from politics; and the opportunism of individuals placing personal profit ahead of public good.

Tacitus observes these issues most patently in the Principate of Tiberius, with both the emperor and his 'creature' Sejanus appearing as the instigators of the problems which Tacitus would experience again under Domitian. Thus in *Annals* IV.2.1, Sejanus is seen to 'increase the previously limited influence of the prefecture [of the Praetorian Guard] by gathering into a single camp the cohorts scattered across the city'. The fact that he has an ulterior motive (*praetendebat*), namely his own political advancement, chafes Tacitus for several of the reasons outlined above, but not least because it reinforces that political power is being acquired and maintained through military force and threat. Thus the army has replaced the Senate as the key political organ. Such a conclusion is reinforced by the death of Cremutius Cordus in AD 25 (*Ann.* IV.34–35), which Seneca (*On Consolation to Marcia*, 22.4–7) expands upon to note that, while formally charged with publishing a history wherein he had praised the assassins of Caesar, his fate actually arose due to Sejanus' resentment of Cremutius' hostile remarks about him.

That such offences could be perpetrated, with the Senate itself powerless or unwilling – due to personal motivations – to prevent them, is perhaps the defining aspect of Tacitus' narrative of the abuse of power under the Tiberian Principate, and particularly Sejanus' role within it.

Annals Book V.1–5 (A-Level sections in English)

Annals Book V opens at the beginning of AD 29, with Tacitus' first observation being the death of Julia Augusta, perhaps better known as Livia, the wife of the emperor Augustus and mother to Tiberius. Tacitus' summary of her life – and her marriage to Augustus – is brief and unflattering, describing her as 'a good match for the qualities of her husband and the hypocrisy of her son' (*Annals* V.1.3).

Gaius Caesar, the next emperor, took charge of the funeral affairs for his great-grandmother, with Tiberius staunchly refusing to leave Capri to attend the ceremony, pleading the 'magnitude of business' (V.2.1). In reality, the relationship between the two of them had been poor for many years, with Tiberius railing against her endeavours to involve herself in politics and exercise her influence over him.

Tacitus marks the death of Livia as something of a watershed moment, claiming that after her death it was 'sheer, oppressive despotism' (V.3.1). Tacitus views Livia as having been a check on both the ambitions of Sejanus and the cruelties of Tiberius, a check which now no longer held sway. Tiberius' immediate action was to move against Agrippina and Nero – further highlighting the factionalism within the imperial family and, more widely, Rome itself.

Factionalism and opportunism, those motifs which are seen in Book IV, come to even greater prominence in the opening chapters of

Book V. The public are seen to be at odds with the Princeps (V.4.2), while Tacitus notes that 'public misfortunes are interpreted by individuals as an opportunity for seeking favour' (V.3.2), and that some are even taking this opportunity to criticize Sejanus himself (V.4.3). But all of this pushed Sejanus onwards, giving him the ammunition to demonstrate to Tiberius that the Senate and People were spurning the wishes of the Emperor. Tacitus' remark that 'no grim deed was done that day' (V.4.3) is ominous in the extreme, foreshadowing the brutality of the reprisals of both Sejanus and Tiberius.

This is perhaps the most telling aspect of those elements of Book V that survive – the text breaks off midway through V.5, with the next sentence relating to matters in AD 31. Thus Tacitus' record of the majority of AD 29, all of AD 30 and most of AD 31 – including Sejanus' downfall – does not survive for us.

Tacitus' style

Tacitus is generally regarded as one of the more challenging Latin Prose authors. This is due to the fact that he deliberately employs the full range of Latin syntax, entailing that there is a beautiful idiosyncrasy to his work. In this brief introduction, some of the more obvious stylistic flourishes and forms are discussed, although there are notes on individual examples throughout the Commentary section.

That which is usually described as *variatio*, is a distinctive trait of Tacitus' prose style. If the Latin prose of Cicero and Livy is dominated by a balance in sentence structure and clause composition, that of Tacitus is characterized by a conscious choice to deliberately avoid balance. Here Tacitus owes a great debt to his antecedent in Roman historiography, Sallust (86–35 BC). The stylistic homages are framed by an equally important thematic parallelism, as Sallust himself had been concerned with the destruction of republican society which he had lived through, publishing his account of Catiline's conspiracy (*Bellum Catilinae*) shortly after the assassination of Julius Caesar in 44 BC. Sallust's disaffection with contemporary society, itself modelled on the disenchanted style of the Greek historian Thucydides (*c.* 460–*c.* 400 BC), resonated with Tacitus, as did the style of Latin which Sallust developed to communicate his sentiment: to put this pithily, disjointed Latin reflected a disjointed society. Thus Sallust revels in archaisms and *variatio*, and it is this style that was followed by Tacitus too.

This may incorporate a number of changes to the expected form of composition in order to keep the reader engaged. These may include, but are not limited to: sentences length, indirect versus direct speech and avoidance of repetition. Thus we see an ablative absolute co-ordinating with an adjective (e.g. *vergente ... senecta secretoque ... mollitum: Ann.* IV.41.2); we see *alii* being followed by *multi ... quidam* (IV.38.4); and we see a preposition + gerundive co-ordinating with an indirect command (*utque ... regimen susciperent*: IV.9.1). These unexpected and in some cases disharmonious arrangements may well have been influenced by Tacitus' own thoughts on oratory and rhetorical style which were dominated by the belief in the need to be witty, incisive, and novel in order to entertain an audience (Tac., *Dialogues* 19–20). However, as indicated above, they may also be deliberately displayed in the Tiberian hexad to highlight the vagaries and uncertainties of the period as he perceived it. Given that we are presented with the themes of hypocrisy, faction and deceit, perhaps the frequency of unexpected phraseology is designed to mirror the overall mood of uncertainty that dominates Tiberius' reign.

This concern for presentation may also account for the dramatic and, at times, almost poetic pattern of Tacitus' Tiberian books and of Book IV in particular. For example, in IV.59 Sejanus seems to adopt the mien of a theatrical impresario, as he *adsimulabat iudicis partes*, while encouraging others to *accusatorum nomina sustinerent*. This theatrical metaphor is mirrored in other elements, such as the frequency of vocabulary dealing with perception (*species, ostendo, occultus, fallo*, etc.), and serves to contribute to a major theme of the Tacitean version of the Tiberian period: the dichotomy between façade and reality.

Here the Tacitean obituary for Tiberius (*Ann.* VI.51.3) becomes increasingly valuable to us in encapsulating our author's thoughts on his subject matter:

> *morum quoque tempora illi diversa: egregium vita famaque quoad privatus vel in imperiis sub Augusto fuit; occultum ac subdolum fingendis virtutibus donec Germanicus ac Drusus superfuere; idem inter bona malaque mixtus incolumi matre; intestabilis saevitia sed obtectis libidinibus dum Seianum dilexit timuitve: postremo in scelera simul ac dedecora prorupit postquam remoto pudore et metu suo tantum ingenio utebatur.*

> In his behaviour too there were differing phases: one exceptional in life and reputation as long as he was a private individual or in commands under Augustus; one secretive and guileful in its fabrication of virtues while Germanicus and Drusus survived; he was simultaneously a blend of good and evil during his mother's lifetime; infamous for his savagery, but with his lusts cloaked, inasmuch as he felt love or fear respectively for Sejanus; lastly he erupted into crimes and degradations alike when at last, with his shame and dread removed, he had only himself to rely on.

> (Trans. Woodman, 2004: 194)

If this is the Tacitean summary of the man, we should perhaps not be surprised by the *variatio* that he employs to present the topsy-turvy politics and morality of the period as our author perceived it. Thus we have deviation from the norm in terms of both behaviour and syntax.

This perhaps accounts for the fact that Tacitus' style has not always been admired. In the seventeenth century, for example, Tacitus was known as the 'Prince of Darkness' ('prince des ténèbres') as a result of the obscurity of his style (Croll, 1966: 86). The style that he deployed certainly played into the often acerbic tone which he wished to adopt.

We must further acknowledge that here we are reading Tacitus' interpretation of events with all the inherent issues that we highlighted above. Therefore, we should not be surprised that Tacitus' opinions frequently manifest in the text in the form of sententiae, short pithy phrases that often serve to round off sections of the text with the author's own opinion of the material that has been presented. These too may be seen as a response to the perceived curbing of free speech under Tiberius, and as Tacitus himself had experienced under Domitian. The attention of the reader is captured with a pointed witticism, but one that seeks to convince the audience of the opinion contained therein.

List of rhetorical terms

akribeia Meaning 'accuracy' or 'exactness', the concept became a key aspect of Greek historiography under Thucydides. Its use conveys the reliability and trustworthiness of the author.

anaphora The repetition of the same word at the beginning of successive clauses for emphasis.

anastrophe The manipulation of the placement of a preposition in a phrase for emphatic effect.

asyndeton The emphatic lack of conjunctions, common between clauses to stress contemporaneity along with other effects.

brachylogy Excessive briefness in speech or writing.

captatio benevolentiae A rhetorical style aimed at soliciting the goodwill of one's audience, often seen at the beginning of a speech or an appeal.

chiasmus Also **chiastic arrangement**. An arrangement or words that is marked by symmetry: e.g. Noun – Adjective – Verb – Adjective – Noun, or A-B-B-A.

The technique is typically deployed by Tacitus where two ideas are of equal significance.

hendiadys Emphatic phraseology where two nouns are linked by a conjunction. Typically one may be converted into an adjective for the other, e.g. *proelium et periculum* – 'danger and battle' – may be rendered as 'dangerous battle'. The term derives from the Greek ἑν δια δυς = 'one through two'.

hyperbole Phraseology that allows for exaggeration for emphatic effect.

juxtaposition The placement of two words or phrases next to one another for contrast or complementary effect.

litotes The use of understatement (often ironic) in order to emphasize the reality of a situation.

metonymy The substitution of the name of an attribute or adjunct for that of the thing meant, for example suit for business executive, or the turf for horse racing.

oratio obliqua The reporting of speech as indirect, being adapted to the point of view, with regard to the person, tense or mood, of the reporter.

oratio recta The words or thoughts of another are quoted unchanged, to emphasize that they are the speaker's own.

polyptoton When different forms (cases, tenses, etc.) of the same word are placed deliberately in sequence for emphatic effect.

polysyndeton Emphatic use of conjunctions, often within a list. Can have multiple effects including, but not limited to, a sense of irresistible accumulation, scale or confusion.

repraesentatio The writer imagines himself as a contemporary and uses tenses appropriate to that point of view.

ring composition An extension of a chiastic arrangement across a whole passage of text, where the end phrasing deliberately recalls the beginning of the section.

sententia Typically the closing remark of a chapter or section, where the phrase stands in apposition with the preceding idea. The technique is used to communicate the author's opinion on events or people, even if this appears as contrary to the material just presented. It may be usefully thought of as the rhetorical 'sting in the tail'.

synonymia The use of synonyms (words similar in meaning) in sequence for emphatic effect.

tricolon An emphatic group of three.

Further reading

Bird, H.W., 1969, 'L. Aelius Seianus and His Political Significance', in
    Latomus, 28, Fasc. 1: 61–98.

Croll, M., 1966, *Style, Rhetoric and Rhythm*, Princeton University Press.

Levick, B., 1986, *Tiberius the Politician*, London.

Marsh, F.B., 1959, *Reign of Tiberius*, Barnes & Noble: New York.

Martin, R.H., 1953, 'Variatio and the Development of Tacitus' Style', in
    Eranos 51: 89–96.

Mellor, R., 1993, *Tacitus*, Routledge: London and New York.

Miller, N.P. (1968), 'Tiberius Speaks: An Examination of the Utterances
    Ascribed to Him in the *Annals* of Tacitus', in *The American Journal of
    Philology* 89: 1–19

Seager, R., 2005, *Tiberius*, Blackwell (Ancient Lives Series).

Shotter, D.C.A., 1974, 'The Fall of Sejanus: Two Problems', in *Classical
    Philology*, Vol.69 No.1: 42–46.

Shotter, D.C.A., 2004, *Tiberius Caesar* (Second Edition), Lancaster
    Pamphlets in Ancient History.

Syme, R., 1958, *Tacitus*, (Two Volumes) Oxford, Clarendon Press.

Woodman, A.J., 1972, 'Remarks on the Structure and Content of Tacitus,
    Annals 4.57-67', in *Classical Quarterly* 22: 150–8.

Woodman, A.J., 1989, 'Tacitus' Obituary of Tiberius', in *Classical Quarterly*
    39: 197–204.

Wharton, D.B., 1997, 'Tacitus' Tiberius: The State of the Evidence for the
    Emperor's *Ipsissima Verba* in the Annals', in *The American Journal of
    Philology*, Vol.118. No.1: 119–125.

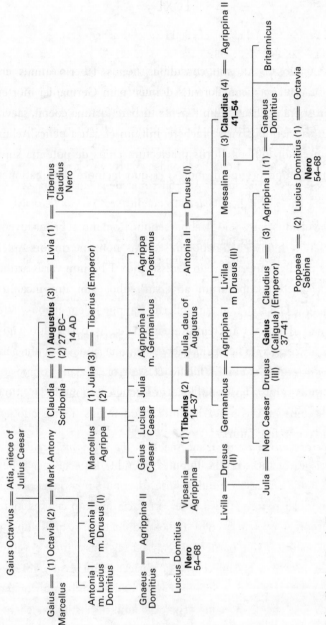

Julio-Claudian Family Tree

Text

1. C. Asinio C. Antistio consulibus nonus Tiberio annus erat compositae rei publicae, florentis domus (nam Germanici mortem inter prospera ducebat), cum repente turbare fortuna coepit, saevire ipse aut saevientibus viris praebere. initium et causa penes Aelium Seianum cohortibus praetoriis praefectum cuius de potentia supra memoravi: nunc originem, mores, et quo facinore dominationem raptum ierit expediam.

genitus Vulsiniis patre Seio Strabone, equite Romano, et prima iuventa   2
C. Caesarem divi Augusti nepotem sectatus, non sine rumore Apicio diviti et prodigo stuprum veno dedisse, mox Tiberium variis artibus devinxit, adeo ut obscurum adversum alios sibi uni incautum intectumque efficeret, non tam sollertia (quippe isdem artibus victus est) quam deum ira in rem Romanam, cuius pari exitio viguit ceciditque. corpus illi laborum tolerans, animus audax; sui obtegens,   3
in alios criminator; iuxta adulatio et superbia; palam compositus pudor, intus summa apiscendi libido, eiusque causa modo largitio et luxus, saepius industria ac vigilantia, haud minus noxiae quotiens parando regno finguntur.

2. vim praefecturae modicam antea intendit, dispersas per urbem cohortes una in castra conducendo, ut simul imperia acciperent numeroque et robore et visu inter se fiducia ipsis, in ceteros metus oreretur. praetendebat lascivire militem diductum; si quid subitum ingruat, maiore auxilio pariter subveniri; et severius acturos si vallum statuatur procul urbis inlecebris. ut perfecta sunt castra, inrepere   2
paulatim militares animos adeundo, appellando; simul centuriones ac tribunos ipse deligere. neque senatorio ambitu abstinebat clientes suos honoribus aut provinciis ornandi, facili Tiberio atque ita prono

A S

ut socium laborum non modo in sermonibus, sed apud patres et populum celebraret colique per theatra et fora effigies eius interque principia legionum sineret.

3.　ceterum plena Caesarum domus, iuvenis filius, nepotes adulti moram cupitis adferebant; et quia vi tot simul corripere intutum, dolus intervalla scelerum poscebat. placuit tamen occultior via et a 2 Druso incipere, in quem recenti ira ferebatur. (nam Drusus impatiens aemuli et animo commotior orto forte iurgio intenderat Seiano manus et contra tendentis os verberaverat.) igitur cuncta temptanti 3 promptissimum visum ad uxorem eius Liviam convertere, quae soror Germanici, formae initio aetatis indecorae, mox pulchritudine praecellebat. hanc ut amore incensus adulterio pellexit et, postquam primi flagitii potitus est (neque femina amissa pudicitia alia abnuerit), ad coniugii spem, consortium regni et necem mariti impulit. atque 4 illa, cui avunculus Augustus, socer Tiberius, ex Druso liberi, seque ac maiores et posteros municipali adultero foedabat ut pro honestis et praesentibus flagitiosa et incerta expectaret. sumitur in conscientiam Eudemus, amicus ac medicus Liviae, specie artis frequens secretis. pellit domo Seianus uxorem Apicatam, ex qua tres liberos genuerat, ne 5 paelici suspectaretur. sed magnitudo facinoris metum, prolationes, diversa interdum consilia adferebat.

4.　interim anni principio Drusus ex Germanici liberis togam virilem sumpsit, quaeque fratri eius Neroni decreverat senatus repetita. addidit orationem Caesar multa cum laude filii sui quod patria benevolentia in fratris liberos foret. nam Drusus (quamquam arduum sit eodem loci potentiam et concordiam esse) aequus adulescentibus aut certe non adversus habebatur.

exin vetus et saepe simulatum proficiscendi in provincias consilium 2 refertur. multitudinem veteranorum praetexebat imperator et dilectibus supplendos exercitus: nam voluntarium militem deesse ac, si suppeditet, non eadem virtute ac modestia agere, quia plerumque inopes ac vagi sponte militiam sumant. percensuitque cursim 3 numerum legionum et quas provincias tutarentur: quod mihi quoque exequendum reor, quae tunc Romana copia in armis, qui socii reges, quanto sit angustius imperitatum.

Chapters 5–6. deal with various pieces of state business including, but not limited to: the disposition of the legions; the types of matters being brought before the Senate; and the shortness of the food supply for the plebs.

7. quae cuncta non quidem comi via sed horridus ac plerumque formidatus retinebat tamen, donec morte Drusi verterentur. nam dum superfuit, mansere, quia Seianus incipiente adhuc potentia bonis consiliis notescere volebat et ultor metuebatur non occultus odii, set crebro querens incolumi filio adiutorem imperii alium vocari. et 2 quantum superesse ut collega dicatur! primas dominandi spes in arduo; ubi sis ingressus, adesse studia et ministros. extructa iam sponte praefecti castra, datos in manum milites, cerni effgiem eius in monimentis Cn. Pompei, communes illi cum familia Drusorum fore nepotes. precandam post haec modestiam ut contentus esset. 3 neque raro neque apud paucos talia iaciebat, et secreta quoque eius corrupta uxore prodebantur.

8. igitur Seianus maturandum ratus deligit venenum, quo paulatim inrepente fortuitus morbus adsimularetur. id Druso datum per Lygdum spadonem, ut octo post annos cognitum est.

ceterum Tiberius per omnes valetudinis eius dies, nullo metu an ut 2 firmitudinem animi ostentaret, etiam defuncto necdum sepulto, curiam ingressus est; consulesque sede vulgari per speciem maestitiae sedentis honoris locique admonuit et effusum in lacrimas senatum victo gemitu, simul oratione continua erexit: non quidem sibi ignarum 3 posse argui quod tam recenti dolore subierit oculos senatus; vix propinquorum adloquia tolerari, vix diem aspici a plerisque lugentium. neque illos imbecillitatis damnandos; se tamen fortiora solacia e complexu rei publicae petivisse. miseratusque Augustae extremam senectam, rudem adhuc nepotum et vergentem aetatem suam, ut Germanici liberi, unica praesentium malorum levamenta, inducerentur petivit. egressi consules firmatos adloquio adulescentulos deductosque 4 ante Caesarem statuunt. quibus adprensis 'patres conscripti, hos' inquit 'orbatos parente tradidi patruo ipsorum precatusque sum, quamquam esset illi propria suboles, ne secus quam suum sanguinem foveret, attolleret, sibique et posteris confirmaret. erepto Druso preces ad vos 5 converto disque et patria coram obtestor: Augusti pronepotes, clarissimis maioribus genitos, suscipite, regite, vestram meamque vicem explete. hi vobis, Nero et Druse, parentum loco: ita nati estis ut bona malaque vestra ad rem publicam pertineant.'

9. magno ea fletu et mox precationibus faustis audita. ac si modum orationi posuisset, misericordia sui gloriaque animos audientium impleverat; ad vana et totiens inrisa revolutus, de reddenda re publica utque consules seu quis alius regimen susciperent, vero quoque et honesto fidem dempsit.

Memoriae Drusi eadem quae in Germanicum decernuntur, plerisque 2 additis, ut ferme amat posterior adulatio. funus imaginum pompa maxime inlustre fuit, cum origo Iuliae gentis Aeneas omnesque Albanorum reges et conditor urbis Romulus, post Sabina nobilitas, Attus Clausus ceteraeque Claudiorum effigies longo ordine spectarentur.

10. in tradenda morte Drusi quae plurimis maximaeque fidei auctoribus memorata sunt rettuli; sed non omiserim eorundem temporum rumorem, validum adeo ut noudum exolescat: corrupta ad 2 scelus Livia Seianum Lygdi quoque spadonis animum stupro vinxisse, quod is aetate atque forma carus domino interque primores ministros

erat; deinde, inter conscios ubi locus veneficii tempusque composita
sint, eo audaciae provectum ut verteret et occulto indicio Drusum
veneni in patrem arguens moneret Tiberium vitandam potionem,
quae prima ei apud filium epulanti offerretur. ea fraude captum 3
senem, postquam convivium inierat, exceptum poculum Druso
tradidisse, atque illo ignaro et iuveniliter hauriente auctam
suspicionem tamquam metu et pudore sibimet inrogaret mortem
quam patri struxerat.

11. haec vulgo iactata, super id quod nullo auctore certo firmantur,
prompte refutaveris. quis enim mediocri prudentia, nedum Tiberius
tantis rebus exercitus, inaudito filio exitium offerret, idque sua manu
et nullo ad paenitendum regressu? quin potius ministrum veneni
excruciaret, auctorem exquireret, insita denique etiam in extraneos
cunctatione et mora adversum unicum et nullius ante flagitii
compertum uteretur? sed quia Seianus facinorum omnium repertor 2
habebatur, ex nimia caritate in eum Caesaris et ceterorum in utrumque
odio quamvis fabulosa et immania credebantur, atrociore semper
fama erga dominantium exitus. ordo alioqui sceleris per Apicatam
Seiani proditus, tormentis Eudemi ac Lygdi patefactus est; neque
quisquam scriptor tam infensus extitit ut Tiberio obiectaret, cum
omnia alia conquirerent intenderentque. mihi tradendi arguendique 3
rumoris causa fuit ut claro sub exemplo falsas auditiones depellerem
peteremque ab iis, quorum in manus cura nostra venerit, <ne>
divulgata atque incredibilia avide accepta veris neque in miraculum
corruptis antehabeant

12. ceterum laudante filium pro rostris Tiberio senatus populusque
habitum ac voces dolentum simulatione magis quam libens
induebat, domumque Germanici revirescere occulti laetabantur.
quod principium favoris et mater Agrippina spem male tegens
perniciem adceleravere. nam Seianus, ubi videt mortem Drusi inultam 2
interfectoribus, sine maerore publico esse, ferox scelerum et quia

prima provenerant, volutare secum quonam modo Germanici liberos
perverteret, quorum non dubia successio. neque spargi venenum
in tres poterat, egregia custodum fide et pudicitia Agrippinae
impenetrabili. igitur contumaciam eius insectari, vetus Augustae   3
odium, recentem Liviae conscientiam exagitare ut superbam
fecunditate, subnixam popularibus studiis inhiare dominationi apud
Caesarem arguerent. atque haec callidis criminatoribus, inter quos 4
delegerat Iulium Postumum, per adulterium Mutiliae Priscae inter
intimos aviae et consiliis suis peridoneum, quia Prisca in animo
Augustae valida anum suapte natura potentiae anxiam insociabilem
nurui efficiebat. Agrippinae quoque proximi inliciebantur pravis
sermonibus tumidos spiritus perstimulare.

Chapters 13–16 see Tacitus ending his account of AD *23 with a number
of domestic items. The items in themselves are a distraction from the
main narrative, serving to build suspense on how Sejanus' plans are
developing.*

Chapters 17–33 cover the year AD *24, with 17–22 covering
political affairs at home, 23–26 discussing the victory over Tacfarinas in
Africa, with 27–31 returning to home affairs, notably the trial of Vibius
Serenus, who had been accused by his own son (also called Vibius
Serenus).*

*Chapters 32–33 serve as a digression from Tacitus on the nature of
writing history, in particular of the dangers of praising free speech.*

Chapters 34–36 mark the opening of AD *24, the most famous section
being the trial of Cremutius Cordus, the historian who was put on trial
for his annalistic history wherein he had praised Brutus and Cassius,
the assassins of Julius Caesar.*

*Chapters 37–38 cover the attitude of Tiberius towards the imperial cult,
which sees the Princeps spurning any cult for himself.*

AS

39.   at Seianus nimia fortuna socors et muliebri insuper cupidine incensus, promissum matrimonium flagitante Livia, componit ad Caesarem codicillos (moris quippe tum erat quamquam praesentem scripto adire). eius talis forma fuit: benevolentia patris Augusti et mox 2 plurimis Tiberii iudiciis ita insuevisse ut spes votaque sua non prius ad deos quam ad principum aures conferret. neque fulgorem honorum umquam precatum: excubias ac labores, ut unum e militibus, pro incolumitate imperatoris malle; ac tamen quod pulcherrimum adeptum, ut coniunctione Caesaris dignus crederetur. hinc initium 3 spei; et quoniam audiverit Augustum in conlocanda filia non nihil etiam de equitibus Romanis consultavisse, ita, si maritus Liviae quaereretur, haberet in animo amicum sola necessitudinis gloria usurum. non enim exuere imposita munia; satis aestimare firmari 4 domum adversum iniquas Agrippinae offensiones, idque liberorum causa: nam sibi multum superque vitae fore quod tali cum principe explevisset.

40.   ad ea Tiberius laudata pietate Seiani suisque in eum beneficiis modice percursis, cum tempus tamquam ad integram consultationem petivisset, adiunxit: ceteris mortalibus in eo stare consilia, quid sibi conducere putent; principum diversam esse sortem, quibus praecipua rerum ad famam derigenda. ideo se non illuc decurrere, quod 2 promptum rescriptu: posse ipsam Liviam statuere, nubendum post Drusum an in penatibus isdem tolerandum haberet; esse illi matrem et aviam, propiora consilia. simplicius acturum, de inimicitiis primum 3 Agrippinae, quas longe acrius arsuras si matrimonium Liviae velut in partes domum Caesarum distraxisset. sic quoque erumpere aemulationem feminarum, eaque discordia nepotes suos convelli; quid si intendatur certamen tali coniugio?

'Falleris enim, Seiane, si te mansurum in eodem ordine putas, et 4 Liviam, quae C. Caesari, mox Druso nupta fuerit, ea mente acturam ut cum equite Romano senescat. ego ut sinam, credisne passuros qui

fratrem eius, qui patrem maioresque nostros in summis imperiis
videre? vis tu quidem istum intra locum sistere; sed illi magistratus et　5
primores, qui te invitum perrumpunt omnibusque de rebus consulunt,
excessisse iam pridem equestre fastigium longeque antisse patris
mei amicitias non occulti ferunt; perque invidiam tui me quoque
incusant. at enim Augustus filiam suam equiti Romano tradere　6
meditatus est. mirum hercule si, cum in omnis curas distraheretur
immensumque attolli provideret quem coniunctione tali super alios
extulisset, C. Proculeium et quosdam in sermonibus habuit insigni
tranquillitate vitae, nullis rei publicae negotiis permixtos! sed si
dubitatione Augusti movemur, quanto validius est quod Marco
Agrippae, mox mihi conlocavit! atque ego haec pro amicitia non　7
occultavi; ceterum neque tuis neque Liviae destinatis adversabor. ipse
quid intra animum volutaverim, quibus adhuc necessitudinibus
immiscere te mihi parem, omittam ad praesens referre; id tantum
aperiam: nihil esse tam excelsum quod non virtutes istae tuusque in
me animus mereantur; datoque tempore vel in senatu vel in contione
non reticebo.'

41.　rursum Seianus non iam de matrimonio, sed altius metuens
tacita suspicionum, vulgi rumorem, ingruentem invidiam deprecatur;
ac ne adsiduos in domum coetus arcendo infringeret potentiam aut
receptando facultatem criminantibus praeberet, huc flexit ut Tiberium
ad vitam procul Roma amoenis locis degendam impelleret. multa　2
quippe providebat: sua in manu aditus litterarumque magna ex parte
se arbitrum fore, cum per milites commearent; mox Caesarem
vergente iam senecta secretoque loci mollitum munia imperii facilius
tramissurum; et minui sibi invidiam adempta salutantum turba,
sublatisque inanibus veram potentiam augeri. igitur paulatim negotia　3
urbis, populi adcursus, multitudinem adfluentium increpat, extollens
laudibus quietem et solitudinem, quis abesse taedia et offensiones ac
praecipua rerum maxime agitari.

Chapters 42–44 cover the end of AD *25, covering senatorial business: three trials (42), three foreign embassies (43), and three obituaries (44).*

Chapter 45 covers the death of the praetor Lucius Piso in Spain.

Chapters 46–51 cover the account of the war in Thrace that was successfully concluded in AD *26 by Poppaeus Sabinus, although its inclusion at this point in the narrative – at the beginning of the year – is perhaps to continue the suspense prior to Tiberius' departure.*

52. at Romae commota principis domo, ut series futuri in Agrippinam exitii inciperet, Claudia Pulchra sobrina eius postulatur accusante Domitio Afro. is recens praetura, modicus dignationis et quoquo facinore properus clarescere, crimen impudicitiae, adulterum Furnium, veneficia in principem et devotiones obiectabat. Agrippina 2 semper atrox, tum et periculo propinquae accensa, pergit ad Tiberium ac forte sacrificantem patri repperit. quo initio invidiae non eiusdem ait mactare divo Augusto victimas et posteros eius insectari. non in effigies mutas divinum spiritum transfusum; se imaginem veram, caelesti sanguine ortam; intellegere discrimen, suscipere sordes. frustra Pulchram praescribi, cui sola exitii causa sit quod Agrippinam stulte prorsus ad cultum delegerit, oblita Sosiae ob eadem adflictae. audita haec raram occulti pectoris vocem elicuere, correptamque 3 Graeco versu admonuit non ideo laedi quia non regnaret. Pulchra et 4 Furnius damnantur; Afer primoribus oratorum additus, divulgato ingenio et secuta adseveratione Caesaris, qua suo iure disertum eum appellavit. mox capessendis accusationibus aut reos tutando prosperiore eloquentiae quam morum fama fuit, nisi quod aetas extrema multum etiam eloquentiae dempsit, dum fessa mente retinet silentii impatientiam.

53. at Agrippina pervicax irae et morbo corporis implicata, cum viseret eam Caesar, profusis diu ac per silentium lacrimis, mox invidiam et preces orditur: subveniret solitudini, daret maritum:

habilem adhuc iuventam sibi, neque aliud probis quam ex matrimonio
solacium; esse in civitate * * * Germanici coniugem ac liberos eius
recipere dignarentur. sed Caesar, non ignarus quantum ex re publica 2
peteretur, ne tamen offensionis aut metus manifestus foret, sine
responso quamquam instantem reliquit. (id ego, a scriptoribus
annalium non traditum, repperi in commentariis Agrippinae filiae,
quae Neronis principis mater vitam suam et casus suorum posteris
memoravit.)

54.   ceterum Seianus maerentem et improvidam altius perculit,
immissis qui per speciem amicitiae monerent paratum ei venenum,
vitandas soceri epulas. atque illa simulationum nescia, cum propter
discumberet, non vultu aut sermone flecti, nullos attingere cibos,
donec advertit Tiberius, forte an quia audiverat. idque quo acrius
experiretur, poma, ut erant adposita, laudans nurui sua manu tradidit.
aucta ex eo suspicio Agrippinae, et intacta ore servis tramisit. nec 2
tamen Tiberii vox coram secuta, sed obversus ad matrem non mirum
ait, si quid severius in eam statuisset, a qua veneficii insimularetur.
inde rumor parari exitium, neque id imperatorem palam audere,
secretum ad perpetrandum quaeri.

Chapters 55–56 cover a senatorial debate that serves as a sequel to IV.3
about the location of a temple for Tiberius in Asia.

57.   inter quae diu meditato prolatoque saepius consilio tandem
Caesar in Campaniam <concessit>, specie dedicandi templa apud
Capuam Iovi, apud Nolam Augusto, sed certus procul urbe degere.
(causam abscessus quamquam secutus plurimos auctorum ad Seiani
artes rettuli, quia tamen caede eius patrata sex postea annos pari
secreto coniunxit, plerumque permoveor num ad ipsum referri verius
sit, saevitiam ac libidinem, cum factis promeret, locis occultantem.
erant qui crederent in senectute corporis quoque habitum pudori 2
fuisse: quippe illi praegracilis et incurva proceritas, nudus capillo

vertex, ulcerosa facies ac plerumque medicaminibus interstincta; et
Rhodi secreto vitare coetus, recondere voluptates insuerat. traditur   3
etiam matris impotentia extrusum, quam dominationis sociam
aspernabatur neque depellere poterat, cum dominationem ipsam
donum eius accepisset. nam dubitaverat Augustus Germanicum,
sororis nepotem et cunctis laudatum, rei Romanae imponere; sed
precibus uxoris evictus Tiberio Germanicum, sibi Tiberium adscivit.
idque Augusta exprobrabat, reposcebat.)

58. profectio arto comitatu fuit: unus senator consulatu functus,
Cocceius Nerva, cui legum peritia; eques Romanus praeter Seianum
ex inlustribus Curtius Atticus; ceteri liberalibus studiis praediti, ferme
Graeci, quorum sermonibus levaretur. ferebant periti caelestium iis   2
motibus siderum excessisse Roma Tiberium ut reditus illi negaretur;
unde exitii causa multis fuit, properum finem vitae coniectantibus
vulgantibusque: neque enim tam incredibilem casum providebant ut
undecim per annos libens patria careret. mox patuit breve confinium   3
artis et falsi, veraque quam obscuris tegerentur. nam in urbem non
regressurum haud forte dictum: ceterorum nescii egere, cum
propinquo rure aut litore et saepe moenia urbis adsidens extremam
senectam compleverit. **59.** ac forte illis diebus oblatum Caesari anceps
periculum auxit vana rumoris, praebuitque ipsi materiem cur
amicitiae constantiaeque Seiani magis fideret. vescebantur in villa,
cui vocabulum Speluncae, mare Amunclanum inter <et> Fundanos
montes, nativo in specu. eius os lapsis repente saxis obruit quosdam
ministros. hinc metus in omnes et fuga eorum qui convivium   2
celebrabant; Seianus genu utroque et manibus super Caesarem
suspensus opposuit sese incidentibus, atque habitu tali repertus est a
militibus qui subsidio venerant. maior ex eo et, quamquam exitiosa
suaderet, ut non sui anxius cum fide audiebatur.

adsimulabatque iudicis partis adversum Germanici stirpem, subditis   3
qui accusatorum nomina sustinerent maximeque insectarentur

Neronem, proximum successioni et, quamquam modesta iuventa, plerumque tamen quid in praesentiarum conduceret oblitum, dum a libertis et clientibus, apiscendae potentiae properis, exstimulatur ut erectum et fidentem animi ostenderet: velle id populum Romanum, cupere exercitus, neque ausurum contra Seianum, qui nunc patientiam senis et segnitiam iuvenis iuxta insultet.

60. haec atque talia audienti nihil quidem pravae cogitationis, sed interdum voces procedebant contumaces et inconsultae, quas adpositi custodes exceptas auctasque cum deferrent neque Neroni defendere daretur, diversae insuper sollicitudinum formae oriebantur. nam 2 alius occursum eius vitare, quidam salutatione reddita statim averti, plerique inceptum sermonem abrumpere, insistentibus contra inridentibusque qui Seiano fautores aderant.

enimvero Tiberius torvus aut falsum renidens vultu: seu loqueretur seu taceret iuvenis, crimen ex silentio, ex voce. ne nox quidem secura, cum uxor vigilias, somnos, suspiria matri Liviae atque illa Seiano patefaceret; qui fratrem quoque Neronis Drusum traxit in partes, spe obiecta principis loci, si priorem aetate et iam labefactum demovisset. atrox Drusi ingenium super cupidinem potentiae et solita fratribus 3 odia accendebatur invidia, quod mater Agrippina promptior Neroni erat. neque tamen Seianus ita Drusum fovebat ut non in eum quoque semina futuri exitii meditaretur, gnarus praeferocem et insidiis magis opportunum.

Chapter 61 covers the end of AD *26, primarily on the deaths of Asinius Agrippa and Quintus Haterius.*

Chapters 62–63 opens the account of AD *27 with the disaster of the collapse of the amphithaetre at Fidenae.*

Chapters 64–65 continue this line with the disaster in Rome of a major fire on the Caelian hill.

A Level

Chapter 66 covers a further example of the prevalence of accusations in Rome, with the account of the case of Quintilius Varus.

67. at Caesar dedicatis per Campaniam templis, quamquam edicto monuisset ne quis quietem eius inrumperet concursusque oppidanorum disposito milite prohiberentur, perosus tamen municipia et colonias omniaque in continenti sita, Capreas se in insulam abdidit, trium milium freto ab extremis Surrentini promunturii diiunctam. solitudinem eius placuisse maxime crediderim, quoniam importuosum circa mare et vix modicis navigiis pauca subsidia; neque adpulerit quisquam nisi gnaro custode. caeli temperies hieme mitis obiectu montis, quo saeva ventorum arcentur; aestas in favonium obversa et aperto circum pelago peramoena; prospectabatque pulcherrimum sinum, antequam Vesuvius mons ardescens faciem loci verteret. Graecos ea tenuisse Capreasque Telebois habitatas fama tradit; sed tum Tiberius duodecim villarum †nominibus et molibus† insederat, quanto intentus olim publicas ad curas, tanto occultior in luxus et malum otium resolutus. manebat quippe suspicionum et credendi temeritas, quam Seianus augere etiam in urbe suetus acrius turbabat non iam occultis adversum Agrippinam et Neronem insidiis. quis additus miles nuntios, introitus aperta, secreta velut in annales referebat; ultroque struebantur qui monerent perfugere ad Germaniae exercitus vel celeberrimo fori effigiem divi Augusti amplecti populumque ac senatum auxilio vocare. eaque spreta ab illis, velut pararent, obiciebantur.

68. Iunio Silano et Silio Nerva consulibus foedum anni principium incessit tracto in carcerem inlustri equite Romano Titio Sabino ob amicitiam Germanici: neque enim omiserat coniugem liberosque eius percolere, sector domi, comes in publico, post tot clientes unus eoque apud bonos laudatus et gravis iniquis. hunc Latinius Latiaris, Porcius Cato, Petilius Rufus, M. Opsius praetura functi adgrediuntur, cupidine consulatus ad quem

non nisi per Seianum aditus; neque Seiani voluntas nisi scelere
quaerebatur.

compositum inter ipsos ut Latiaris, qui modico usu Sabinum
contingebat, strueret dolum, ceteri testes adessent, deinde accusationem
inciperent. igitur Latiaris iacere fortuitos primum sermones, mox   3
laudare constantiam, quod non, ut ceteri, florentis domus amicus
adflictam deseruisset; simul honora de Germanico Agrippinam
miserans disserebat. et postquam Sabinus (ut sunt molles in calamitate
mortalium animi) effudit lacrimas, iunxit questus, audentius iam
onerat Seianum, saevitiam, superbiam, spes eius; ne in Tiberium
quidem convicio abstinet. iique sermones, tamquam vetita miscuissent,   4
speciem artae amicitiae fecere. ac iam ultro Sabinus quaerere Latiarem,
ventitare domum, dolores suos quasi ad fidissimum deferre.

69. consultant quos memoravi, quonam modo ea plurium auditu
acciperentur: nam loco, in quem coibatur, servanda solitudinis facies;
et si pone fores adsisterent, metus visus, sonitus aut forte ortae
suspicionis erat. tectum inter et laquearia tres senatores haud minus
turpi latebra quam detestanda fraude sese abstrudunt, foraminibus et
rimis aurem admovent. interea Latiaris repertum in publico Sabinum,   2
velut recens cognita narraturus, domum et in cubiculum trahit
praeteritaque et instantia, quorum adfatim copia, ac novos terrores
cumulat. eadem ille et diutius, quanto maesta, ubi semel prorupere,
difficilius reticentur.

properata inde accusatio, missisque ad Caesarem litteris ordinem   3
fraudis suumque ipsi dedecus narravere. non alias magis anxia et
pavens civitas, <cautissime> agens adversum proximos: congressus,
conloquia, notae ignotaeque aures vitari; etiam muta atque inanima,
tectum et parietes circumspectabantur.

70. sed Caesar sollemnia incipientis anni kalendis Ianuariis epistula
precatus, vertit in Sabinum, corruptos quosdam libertorum et petitum

se arguens, ultionemque haud obscure poscebat. nec mora quin decerneretur; et trahebatur damnatus, quantum obducta veste et adstrictis faucibus niti poterat, clamitans sic inchoari annum, has Seiano victimas cadere. quo intendisset oculos, quo verba acciderent, 2 fuga, vastitas: deseri itinera, fora. et quidam regrediebantur ostentabantque se rursum, id ipsum paventes quod timuissent: quem 3 enim diem vacuum poena, ubi inter sacra et vota, quo tempore verbis etiam profanis abstineri mos esset, vincla et laqueus inducantur? non imprudentem Tiberium tantam invidiam adisse; quaesitum meditatumque, ne quid impedire credatur quo minus novi magistratus, quomodo delubra et altaria, sic carcerem recludant.

secutae insuper litterae grates agentis quod hominem infensum rei 4 publicae punivissent, adiecto trepidam sibi vitam, suspectas inimicorum insidias, nullo nominatim compellato; neque tamen dubitabatur in Neronem et Agrippinam intendi.

71. (ni mihi destinatum foret suum quaeque in annum referre, avebat animus antire statimque memorare exitus quos Latinus atque Opsius ceterique flagitii eius repertores habuere, non modo postquam C. Caesar rerum potitus est sed incolumi Tiberio, qui scelerum ministros, ut perverti ab aliis nolebat, ita plerumque satiatus et oblatis in eandem operam recentibus veteres et praegraves adflixit. verum has atque alias sontium poenas in tempore trademus.) tum censuit Asinius Gallus, 2 cuius liberorum Agrippina matertera erat, petendum a principe ut metus suos senatui fateretur amoverique sineret. nullam aeque Tiberius, 3 ut rebatur, ex virtutibus suis quam dissimulationem diligebat: eo aegrius accepit recludi quae premeret. sed mitigavit Seianus, non Galli amore verum ut cunctationes principis opperiretur, gnarus lentum in meditando, ubi prorupisset, tristibus dictis atrocia facta coniungere.

Per idem tempus Iulia mortem obiit, quam neptem Augustus 4 convictam adulterii damnaverat proieceratque in insulam Trimerum, haud procul Apulis litoribus. illic viginti annis exilium toleravit Augustae ope sustentata, quae florentes privignos cum per occultum subvertisset, misericordiam erga adflictos palam ostentabat.

Chapters 72–73 deal with foreign affairs, primarily the Frisian revolt.

74. clarum inde inter Germanos Frisium nomen, dissimulante Tiberio damna ne cui bellum permitteret. neque senatus in eo cura, an imperii extrema dehonestarentur: pavor internus occupaverat animos, cui remedium adulatione quaerebatur. ita, quamquam 2 diversis super rebus consulerentur, aram clementiae, aram amicitiae effigiesque circum Caesaris ac Seiani censuere; crebrisque precibus efflagitabant, visendi sui copiam facerent. non illi tamen in urbem aut 3 propinqua urbi degressi sunt; satis visum omittere insulam et in proximo Campaniae aspici. eo venire patres, eques, magna pars plebis, anxii erga Seianum, cuius durior congressus atque eo per ambitum et societate consiliorum parabatur. satis constabat auctam ei adrogantiam 4 foedum illud in propatulo servitium spectanti: quippe Romae sueti discursus, et magnitudine urbis incertum quod quisque ad negotium pergat: ibi campo aut litore iacentes nullo discrimine noctem ac diem iuxta gratiam aut fastus ianitorum perpetiebantur, donec id quoque vetitum. et revenere in urbem trepidi, quos non sermone, non visu 5 dignatus erat, quidam male alacres, quibus infaustae amicitiae gravis exitus imminebat

75. ceterum Tiberius neptem Agrippinam, Germanico ortam, cum coram Cn. Domitio tradidisset, in urbe celebrari nuptias iussit. in Domitio super vetustatem generis propinquum Caesaribus sanguinem delegerat: nam is aviam Octaviam et per eam Augustum avunculum praeferebat.

Commentary Notes

1–4 (AD 23)

The beginning of Book IV is very much seen as the beginning of a new phase in Tiberius' reign, marked by the prominence of Sejanus in the political sphere. The narrative for AD 23 focusses almost exclusively on domestic politics within Rome herself, largely ignoring foreign affairs, with the ambitions of Sejanus serving as the focal point.

As the relationships between members of the imperial family are paramount in Book IV a basic family tree (stemma) is appended to the Introduction section on page 24.

1.1

C. Asinio C. Antistio consulibus: 'with Gaius Asinius and Gaius Antistius as consuls'. The book begins with an Ablative Absolute expressing the consular year. This is Tacitus' preferred method of presenting the consular year, and the use of the construction serves a distinctive purpose. By grammatically separating the clause from the main body of the sentence, Tacitus mirrors in his syntax the limited political influence and importance of the consuls themselves. This is particularly effective in this instance, given the following immediate mention on Tiberius' ninth year in power. We are left in little doubt that the consuls themselves serve as nothing more than a vestige of an all-but-forgotten republic. C. Asinius Pollio was the son of Asinius Gallus, who had marked himself out as one of the few outspoken members of the Senate in the early years of Tiberius' reign (see *Annals* I.12.2, for his remarks in the initial senatorial meeting of Tiberius' reign).

nonus Tiberio annus erat: 'it was the ninth year [in power] for Tiberius' – the abrupt transition into this phrase marks where lies the true power in the state. Having succeeded Augustus in AD 14, Tiberius' ninth year of rule would have actually begun in AD 22, but the ascription by Tacitus is deliberate in order to stress that this is to be seen as a new phase of the reign.

compositae rei publicae: 'the state being well-ordered' – a strangely positive phrase from Tacitus for the Tiberian administration. However, its inclusion is designed to elicit a sense of 'the calm before the storm', being contrasted with the succeeding **turbare** ('to place in turmoil'). The section is highly evocative of the disruption that Sejanus brings to the state, from Tacitus' perspective at least.

florentis domus: 'his household flourishing' – nothing could actually have been farther from the truth (as the following remark in parentheses details). The imperial family at this time had been damaged by the death of Germanicus, Tiberius' adopted son, as the death was suspicious at the very least and had caused a rift between Tiberius and Germanicus' widow, Agrippina. The resultant factions within both the family and Rome's aristocracy are a hallmark of the period in Tacitus' presentation of it.

nam Germanici mortem inter prospera ducebat: this is the first of a series of *sententiae* in the prescribed text: 'For he counted the death of Germanicus among the fortunate things.' Here Tacitus ascribes thoughts to Tiberius for which he gives no real evidence. This is perhaps more reflective of Tacitus' own interpretation of events and his usual cynicism than it is of the reality. The major account of the death and funeral process of Germanicus, including the associated trial of Piso, is that of Tacitus himself (*Annals* II.59–III.19 *passim*). In that section Tacitus is at pains to demonstrate the degree to which Tiberius' slight level of mourning is entirely at odds with that of the rest of the Roman state, even going so far as to intimate that Tiberius may have had an indirect hand in the death of his adopted son. However, he was certainly responsible for removing Germanicus from his popularity base in Germany, especially among the troublesome Mainz legions (see *Annals* II.5.1), and sending him to settle issues in the eastern areas of the empire. Hence this observation is entirely in keeping with the character of Tiberius as Tacitus has presented it. It should be noted that Velleius Paterculus (*History of Rome* II.130.3), who very much presents the official imperial version of events, counts the death of Germanicus in AD 19 among Tiberius' misfortunes.

rei publicae . . . domus: note the use of the two genitives after **nonus annus** ('a ninth year of . . .') to define the two concrete areas of Tiberius' world: public and private.

cum repente turbare fortuna coepit, saevire ipse: 'when fortune began to turn tumultuous, and the man himself savage' – a good example of the inverted *cum* clause, i.e. where what should be grammatically subordinate carries the main idea of the sentence, hence the verb in the Indicative Mood. Here the focus is decidedly placed upon the turmoil that has begun to affect the state with the appearance of Sejanus. The adverb **repente** ('suddenly') adds to the presentation of this as being unforeseen.

The entire phrase is a clever Tacitean re-working of the Sallustian remark (*Cat.* 10.1) on how the destruction of Carthage actually marked the point of deterioration of the qualities of the Roman state: *saevire fortuna ac miscere omnia coepit* ('Fortune became savage and began to confuse all things'). Here we should note the transfer of *saevitia* ('savagery') from the abstract force of Fortune to the emperor himself, reinforcing that this was Tiberius' own doing, as he moved further and further towards the demeanour of a tyrant. It could also reflect the change in the nature of politics under the Principate, as the fortune of the Princeps himself was now synonymous with that of the state as a whole. The sense of the turmoil arising from within is also marked by the adaptation of *miscere* ('to confuse') to **turbare** ('to throw into turmoil').

saeventibus: the rise of 'savage men' is a frequent occurrence in the six Tiberian books of the *Annals*, typically associated with the accusers (*delatores*) in *maiestas* trials (see Introduction, pp. 1–24). The **polyptoton** here further reinforces the brutality of the period, as does the chiastic arrangement of **saevire ... praebere** ('to be savage ... to provide').

initium et causa: 'beginning and cause' – the emphatic synonymia leaves us in no doubt as to where Tacitus ascribes the blame for these developments.

penes: 'rested with/lay in the house of' + accusative – this preposition is typically found in verse and is the first feature that speaks towards the dramatic and vivid manner in which Tacitus presents Sejanus in the Book. It may be seen in contrast with *domus* above, as if the House of Sejanus is actively seeking to topple the imperial household.

cohortibus praetoriis praefectum: 'Prefect for the Praetorian Cohorts' – the official position that Sejanus held. The Praetorian Cohorts served as the bodyguard of the emperor and were among the very few troops allowed inside the city of Rome. They come to be seen by Tacitus as a symbol of the oppression that the Principate could exert.

cuius de potentia supra memoravi: 'about whose power I have made mention above' – Tacitus has made passing reference to Sejanus before Book IV. The most pertinent for this remark is at *Annals* I.24.2 where Sejanus is described as 'enjoying great influence with Tiberius' when he is appointed Praetorian Prefect in AD 14.

originem, mores: These are two of the traditional areas of focus for ancient biography, translating as 'background' and 'character' respectively. The fact that Tacitus goes to such lengths to introduce his biographical presentation of Sejanus, to say nothing of the length of the excursus itself, reinforces how significant a figure Sejanus is seen to be in the Tiberian period.

quo facinore: 'by what crime' – *facinus* may be translated as either 'deed' or 'crime', with the pejorative usage typically informed more by context in Tacitus. Here, given that it is juxtaposed with *dominatio* ('absolute power'), the negative interpretation is made clear: Sejanus is willing to use any means necessary to acquire power.

raptum: 'to snatch' – Supine after a verb of motion (**ierit**) to express Purpose.

1.2

Vulsiniis: Vulsinii (modern Bolsena), located in the ancient region of Etruria.

Seio Strabone: Lucius Seius Strabo, a Roman *eques* who was Praetorian Guard commander at the time of Tiberius' accession in AD 14. He shared this post with his son, Sejanus, only until AD 15, when Strabo was appointed as governor of Egypt. We should remember that Augustus had established Egypt as a special imperial province, one which was governed by an *eques* who reported to the emperor directly. Senators had to seek permission from the emperor in order to visit Egypt (cf. *Annals*, II.59.3).

C. Caesarem ... sectatus: 'was in the train of Gaius Caesar' – Gaius Caesar, grandson of Augustus, son of Marcus Agrippa and Augustus' daughter Julia, b. 20 BC; d. AD 4. Along with his brother Lucius, these young men were seen as would-be successors to Augustus and were

AS

formally adopted by him in that capacity. Both died early and ended the hopes of Augustus for a successor of his own blood. Tacitus (*Annals*, I.3.3) tells us that both were 'carried off by fatefully early deaths or by the guile of their stepmother Livia.' The significance of Gaius being mentioned here is to suggest that Sejanus is very much a political weathervane, aligning himself to whichever individual seems to be in the ascendancy. Thus we are forced to question the sincerity of his loyalty.

non sine rumore: 'not without rumour' – Rumour is an interesting concept in Tacitus and he frequently reports popular rumour in order to then profess that he disbelieves it (e.g. *Annals* IV.10.1: *sed non omiserim eorundem temporem rumorem*, 'I would not leave out a rumour of those times'). His reason for including such content is primarily for insinuation, i.e. it allows him to blacken the character of certain individuals by reflecting the contemporary view of them, while at the same time taking the moral high ground as a historian by claiming that he personally is unconvinced.

stuprum: 'illicit sex' – a highly suggestive word in Latin, that covers a range of deviant sexual activity. Here it has the connotation that Sejanus sold himself to Apicius as a lover, a rent-boy if you will. The Roman view was that the passive sexual partner (he that 'suffered as a woman', *muliebria pati*) was open to condemnation. Thus homosexuality in and of itself was not an issue, but rather sexual passivity. The fact that Sejanus has committed such an act for money (**veno dedisse**) is to be seen not only as particularly degrading, but also as further evidence for his utter lack of scruples in furthering his own career.

mox: 'subsequently' – rather than 'soon', **mox** here connotes the sense of 'the next in a series of suspect behaviour', building upon the idea of **prima iuventa** ('in his early youth') above to create a catalogue of misdeeds.

AS

Tiberium variis artibus devinxit, adeo ut: 'he bound Tiberius by various arts so closely that . . .' – here the **adeo** ('so closely') is qualifying the entire clause rather than just the sense of the verb. The effect is one that communicates the sense of the ensnaring of Tiberius rather well. Tacitus' use of the verb *devincire* ('to bind') is only ever metaphorical, but provokes thoughts of enslavement.

obscurum adversum alios sibi uni incautum intectumque: '. . . he was unfathomable towards others, [but] unguarded and frank to him [Sejanus] alone . . .' – a superb phrase that summarizes much of both Tacitus' style and his opinions on Tiberius. We should note the variatio (see Introduction, pages 17–18) of **adversum** + Acc. and the Dative **sibi uni**, here emphasized by the chiastic arrangement, which fully communicates the polarized outcomes of Sejanus' ensnaring of Tiberius. For more on Tacitus' views on the secrecy, hypocrisy and deceitfulness of Tiberius, see the Introduction (pages 4–8).

sollertia: 'shrewdness' – a trait shared by both Tiberius and Sejanus and reinforces the link between them. The word is also evocative of the degree of political scheming that dominated this period.

quippe isdem artibus vinctus est: 'for in fact he was defeated by the same arts' – very much communicates Tacitus' sense of the 'poetic justice' that will eventually befall Sejanus. This is suggested by the repetition of **artibus**. The use of *vincere* ('to defeat'), along with **intectum** above (deriving from *integere* – 'to be uncovered'), is suggestive that Tacitus wanted to employ militaristic vocabulary in this section, perhaps to suggest the idea of a hidden form of civil war.

deum ira in rem Romanam: 'the anger of the gods against the Roman state' – this is not really a religious statement on Tacitus' part, rather it is a stylistic device designed to emphasize just how destructive to Rome the actions of Sejanus were. This sense of hyperbole is further

AS

heightened by the use of the archaic Genitive Plural **deum**, in place of *deorum*.

cuius pari exitio viguit ceciditque: 'for which his flourishing and fall were equally destructive'. **exitio** here is the Ablative of Attendance, i.e. 'accompanied by whose equal destruction ...'. The antecedent for the Relative Pronoun here is therefore **rem Romanam**. Tacitus here once again states that no matter what Sejanus' actions, he brought destruction to Rome.

1.3

illi: 'his' – Possessive Dative, used when emphasis is laid on the thing possessed, not the possessor. Unsurprising in its appearance here as it introduces a list of Sejanus' qualities.

corpus . . . laborum tolerans: 'a body tolerant of hardships' – while at first sight this may seem a positive, Tacitus is here using it to reinforce just how much Sejanus can endure in his aim to acquire power.

animus audax: 'a bold mind' – **audax** is a politically loaded term, often equated with those individuals who are radicals or revolutionaries.

in alios criminator: 'an accuser against others' – again here we could note the *variatio* of the agent noun (**criminator**) with the earlier participle (**obtegens**), coupled with that between the Genitive **sui** and the Preposition + Acc. (**in alios**). The entire phrase speaks towards his contrary behaviour, with **criminator** again evoking the memory of the maiestas trials (see Introduction, page 3).

iuxta adulatio et superbia: 'flattery side by side with arrogance' – again these Nominatives are dependent on the earlier **illi**, i.e. 'He had ...'. The promotion of the Adverb **iuxta** here communicates the fact that both characteristics are equally visible in Sejanus, i.e. apparent servility to his superiors, and arrogance towards his inferiors.

palam ... intus: 'publicly ... internally' – a very pleasing antithesis which fully communicates the deceitful nature of Sejanus. Outwardly he has **compositus pudor** ('composed modesty') but inside he has **summa apiscendi libido** ('a lust of acquiring the greatest things').

summa apiscendi libido: 'a lust of acquiring the greatest things'. **summa** is Neuter Plural Accusative, serving as the Object of the Gerund **apiscendi**. As is common, here the Genitive Gerund follows an abstract noun (**libido**), i.e. 'a lust of acquiring'. Tacitus is also here using the archaic form *apiscor* in place of *adipiscor* ('to acquire/to obtain'); the effect is vivid and makes Sejanus' lust seem all the more powerful.

eius causa: 'and because of that'. The postposition **causa** (+ Genitive) here allows Tacitus to introduce aspects of Sejanus' behaviour that derive from his lust for power. **eius** refers to his **summa apiscendi libido**.

modo ... saepius: 'at times ... more often' – again *variatio*, here of Temporal Adverbs.

largitio et luxus ... industria ac vigilantia: 'lavish generosity and luxury ... hard work and watchfulness'. Again note the *variatio* on the conjunctions **et** and **ac**. The former pairing generally denote qualities that Tacitus sees as negative in people, whereas the latter pair are normally used more positively although that is not the case here.

haud minus noxiae: 'no less harmful [qualities] ...'. Here we need to understand the sense of *quam* **largitio et luxus** ('than lavish generosity and luxury') in order to complete the comparison. **noxiae** is Feminine Plural in order to agree with both **industria** and **vigilantia**.

AS

parando regno: 'for the obtaining of power'. Here we have the Gerundive **parando**. It is placed in the Dative Case to express Purpose.

finguntur: 'they are feigned'. A very pleasing verb to end this section on the character of Sejanus. The verb is one of a category of words that Tacitus employs in order to create the idea of deceit being dominant in Rome at this time (see Introduction, pages 14–16).

2.1

vim praefecturae: 'the power of the prefectship'. The command of the Praetorian Guard was Sejanus' only real position at this time, so Tacitus makes much of the ways in which he exploited its powers and increased them.

una in castra: 'into one camp'. Note the anastrophe to stress the gathering together of the cohorts.

conducendo: 'by gathering together'. The Ablative Gerund here is used with an instrumental function, i.e. 'he increased the power of the prefectship by gathering together the cohorts . . .'.

ut . . . imperia acciperent . . .: 'so that they might receive orders . . .'. acciperent in the Subjunctive here for the Purpose Clause, as is oreretur. We are led to think that the first, far more simple half of the clause, is the public reason, whereas the second is the far more intricate secret purpose of Sejanus.

numero et robore et visu inter se: 'by their number and their strength and by the mutual sight of one another'. Note the tricolon here, along with the polysyndeton. The three instrumental ablatives here are the factors by which Sejanus hope that the Praetorians will be able to become more politically significant.

ut . . . fiducia ipsis, in ceteros metus oreretur: 'so that confidence in themselves, but fear [of them] in others, might arise'. This is the outcome that Sejanus wishes, and his reason for gathering the cohorts together. The chiastic arrangement serves to mark the linked, but contrasting, outcomes – as does the *variatio* on **ipsis ~ in ceteros**.

praetendebat: 'he alleged' – note the promotion of the verb to the beginning of the clause for emphasis. The vocabulary is again evocative of the duplicity of Sejanus (see Introduction, pages 9–10).

militem: 'soldiery'. The use of the collective singular (in place of the Acc. Pl. *milites*) is perhaps deliberate on the part of Tacitus to communicate the apparently noble intentions of Sejanus, giving a sense of grandeur to his 'public' motivation for the Praetorian camp.

si quid subitum ingruat: 'if anything sudden occurred . . .'. Here we lapse into Indirect Speech, as Tacitus presents the arguments that Sejanus would have done. The verb in this clause should really be in the Imperfect Subjunctive (*ingrueret*), following the introductory **praetendebat**, if we were to observe strict Sequence of Tenses. However, the appearance of the Present Subjunctive is most likely designed to make the speech ascribed to the original speaker appear more graphic. Likewise the euphemistic quality to **quid subitum** ('anything sudden'), combined with its indefinite nature, is suggestive of the fact that this is just an excuse.

pariter subveniri: 'with the support all together'. This is actually an astoundingly bold compression of the Latin, standing for a full phrase in the form of *si pariter miles subvenisset* – 'if the soldiery supported all together'. Tacitus has also replaced the expected, if uncommon, Future Passive Infinitive (*subventurum iri*) with the more graphic Present Passive Infinitive.

procul urbis inlecebris: 'far from the attractions of the city' **procul** + Ablative of Separation. The word **procul** may, but does not have to, refer to a great distance. Thus Sejanus' use of the word here is cunning, and Tacitus' tone with its choice sarcastic. The new Praetorian camp was actually built into the city walls, so they are hardly removed from the distractions of the metropolis.

ut: here + Indicative, thus to be translated as 'when'. It could also suggest 'as soon as'; thus Sejanus' attempts to ingratiate himself with the soldiery begin as soon as he has an effective base of operations.

inrepere: 'he was creeping in'. Historic Infinitive (i.e. a Present Infinitive that is translated as if it were an Imperfect tense verb). Often it is used to impart vividness to the action, as it can 'describe an unfolding scene' (*NLS* §21). Tacitus typically uses *inrepo* of secret or clandestine actions, associating it with plotting and manipulation.

adeundo, appellando: 'by approaching [them], by calling [them] by name'. Here two Gerunds in the Ablative express the means by which Sejanus seeks to ingratiate himself with the soldiers. We should supply (hereafter marked sc.) *eos* as the Object.

ipse deligere: 'he chose ... himself'. Note the archaism *deligo*, which Tacitus prefers to the more usual *eligo*.

neque senatorio ambitu abstinebat ... ornandi: 'Nor did he refrain from courting popularity among the senators by honouring ...'. Here **senatorio** is the equivalent of *apud senatores*. **ornandi** is the Genitive Gerund.

clientes: 'clients'. The concept of the patron~client relationship is the social glue of Rome, creating reciprocal relationships between the classes. Here though there is a cutting irony to the fact that Sejanus, an eques, has senators as his clients. The inversion of the usual social order is typical of Tacitus' presentation of Tiberian Rome: a world where the normal social and moral conventions have been usurped.

facili Tiberio atque ita prono ut: 'With Tiberius being compliant and so well-disposed that ...'. Here Tacitus uses an Ablative Absolute to transition into the Consecutive Clause. The Ablative Absolute also serves as an appendix to the previous clause and this is a typical feature of Tacitus' style, typically where he wishes to be suggestive. Here Tiberius is introduced in a subservient position, which reaches its climax in the details of the ensuing Consecutive Clause.

2.3

socium laborum: 'ally of his labours'. See also 7.1 where Sejanus is described as **adiutorem imperii** (assistant in power). The phraseology is emphatic of the pre-eminent position which Sejanus now enjoyed, with the title of *adiutor* being used by both Velleius Paterculus (127.3) and Dio (LVII.19.7) to describe the role that he filled.

patres et populum: 'senators and people'. The plosive alliteration is necessarily emphatic; with the archaic **patres** perhaps being deliberately chosen to reflect Sejanus' usurpation of long-standing traditions of power.

effigies eius: 'statues of him'. Notice the hyperbaton in the clause, with this phrase being placed between **per theatra et fora** and **inter principia legionum**, reflecting the centrality of Sejanus to public and army life.

3.1

ceterum: 'But as for the rest ...'. Effectively serving as a conjunction to contrast the primacy of Sejanus' public presence with the actual impediments to his acquiring primacy in the succession.

iuvenis filius: 'a youthful son'. Drusus (II), the son of Tiberius, born in 14/13 BC and thus now in his mid-30s.

nepotes adulti: 'adult grandsons'. Nero and Drusus (III), the two elder sons of Germanicus, born in AD 6 and 7 respectively. Additionally,

AS

there was Gaius – Germanicus' youngest son – and the two sons of Drusus (II) – Germanicus and Tiberius Gemellus. The phrasing here, with its emphatic adjectives **iuvenis** and **adulti**, reinforces the scale of Sejanus' ambitions given how many individuals stand between him and the imperial throne.

et quia ... poscebat: 'and because it was unsafe to destroy so many at the same time by force, his trickery demanded intervals between crimes'. There is much emphasis added to this remark, with the contrast between **dolus** and **intutum**, and that between **simul corripere** and **intervalla secelerum**. The overall effect is chiastic and serves to emphasize both Sejanus' ambition and his devious cunning.

placuit tamen occultior via: 'but a yet more secret course pleased him ...'. **tamen** here contrasts **occultior** with **dolus** in the previous clause. The effect is striking to suggest that Sejanus delighted in the most arcane plot imaginable.

impatiens aemuli: 'intolerant of his rival'. A simple phrase that reinforces the factionalism that was rampant at the imperial court at this time. Sejanus is not alone in attempting to exploit the Principate for personal gain, but rather he is the most adept at navigating the currents of power.

intenderat Seiano manus et ... os verberaverat: 'had raised his hands to Sejanus and ... had struck his face'. While Sejanus is seen as the primary actor, Drusus' violence here is used to contrast the direct action of physical confrontation with the devious scheming of Sejanus.

3.3

cuncta temptanti: 'for a man trying everything'. Again, emphatic of the scale of Sejanus' ambition.

Liviam: The daughter of Drusus (I) and therefore niece to Tiberius. She was the wife of Drusus (II) and is typically referred to as Livilla, to differentiate her from Livia, the wife of Augustus and mother of Tiberius.

ut amore incensus: 'as if enflamed by love'. The deception and falsity here is obvious and Tacitus uses it to speak of the utter immorality of Sejanus in his pursuit of power.

postquam primi flagitii potitus est: 'after he obtained this first scandal'. Plosive alliteration and the brevity of the phrase serve to emphasize the efficiency of the action, with *flagitium* speaking of sexual outrage.

neque femina amissa pudicitia alia abnuerit: 'and the woman did not refuse other things once her modesty had been lost'. **abnuerit** here is past potential subjunctive, referring to the likeliest action in the past (*NLS* §120), probably reflecting Tacitus' use of repraesentatio, accounting for why the pluperfect is not used.

femina here is not used in a general sense, but rather specifically refers to Livilla. The dismissive tone achieved is perhaps reflective of Sejanus' own opinion of Livilla as a disposable tool.

Here Tacitus is almost certainly alluding to Livy I.58.7 and the famous remark made by Lucretia: *quid enim salvi est mulieri amissa pudicitia*? ('For what good is left to a woman when her modesty has been lost?'). Whilst for Lucretia her rape was an outrage that required her suicide, Livilla will seek to exploit her own moral outrage to gain political power. The inversion of moral order and the befoulment of Roman identity is a major concern for Tacitus in the reign of Tiberius.

ad coniugi spem, consortium regni et necem mariti: 'to the hope of marriage, partnership of sovereignty, and the death of her husband'.

Simply calling this a tricolon fundamentally limits the complex syntax of Tacitus, where he arranges three elements into two overlapping arrangements where **coniugi spem consortium regni** is chiastic, but yet **consortium regni et necem mariti** is parallel; therefore **coniugi spem ... necem mariti** are again chiastic. This arrangement is highly evocative of not only the overlapping ambitions of Sejanus and Livilla, but also the intricacy of the conspiracy itself.

avunculus ... socer ... liberi: 'great uncle ... father-in-law ... children'. The tricolon here reinforces the scale of Livilla's betrayal of her family.

seque ac maiores et posteros: 'herself and her ancestors and her descendants'. A second tricolon, coupled with polysyndeton, communicates the outrage and infamy of Livilla.

municipali adultero: 'a provincial adulterer'. Highly pejorative. This again is typical of Tacitus' rather snobbish attitude, but also speaks towards standards of Roman political invective, where an individual's social background is ripe for criticism.

ut pro honestis ... incerta exspectaret: 'in order to wait for disgraceful and uncertain things in place of what was honourable and tangible'. The reversal of normal moral values is a consistent theme for Tacitus in his account of the Julio-Claudian period. Note the parallel arrangement of the clause to stress Livilla's conscious exchange of the 'good' for the 'bad'. Livilla's choice here is very surprising given that she was *already* married to the heir presumptive.

Eudemus: A Greek doctor, thus with privileged access at the court; see **frequens secretis** below.

specie artis: 'on the pretext of his skill'. *species* fits into a corpus of vocabulary which Tacitus uses, along with *facies* ('false show'), *imago* and *simulatio* (among others), to communicate the duplicity and falsity of Roman society at this time, with the imperial court as the epicentre.

3.5

pellit domo: 'he forced her from their home'. The promoted verb puts stress on Sejanus' actions. While the date of this action is uncertain, the callousness is overt. This is especially true given that Apicata had already given birth to two sons and a daughter (**tres liberos**), all of whom were killed in AD 31 after Sejanus' downfall.

ne paelici suspectaretur: 'lest he be suspected by his mistress'. **paelici** here is most likely Dative of Agent, although the usage would be unusual. The noun *paelicus*, as it is applied to Livilla, is decidedly pejorative and again seems to be written as if from Sejanus' own perspective.

facinoris: 'crime'. The *facinus* here is the proposed murder of Drusus (II).

4.1

anni principio: 'at the outset of the year'. i.e. AD 23. The explanation for this remark is that the content of chapters 1–3 either preceded AD 23, or alluded to subsequent events. Tacitus now resumes his usual annalistic style (see below on 71.1).

Drusus ex Germanici liberis: 'Drusus from the children of Germanicus'. The specification distinguishes this Drusus from Tiberius' own son. However, the designation also serves to remind the reader of the factionalism of which the death of Germanicus was symptomatic.

quaeque fratri eius Neroni decreverat senatus repitita: '. . . and those things which the Senate had decreed for his brother Nero were now repeated'. *Annals* III.29.1 refers to the assumption of the toga of manhood (*toga virilis*) by Nero on 7 June AD 20. Nero had been born in AD 6 and, after Tiberius' own son, was the most obvious choice for a successor. The advancement of the sons of Germanicus is perhaps to be seen here as making their removal even more pressing from Sejanus' perspective.

patria benevolentia: 'paternal benevolence'. Ablative of Description (Internal Quality) (*NLS* §83). Upon the death of Germanicus, the care of his children passed to Drusus (II).

quamquam arduum sit . . . esse: 'although it is difficult for power and harmony to exist together in the same place'. A cutting remark, indicative of Tacitus' use of *sententia* (see Introduction, page 22). The inclusion of the words *potentia* and *concordia* and their juxtaposition is interesting, as it highlights a fundamental issue at the heart of the Principate, namely that where power rests solely in the hands of a single individual, competition for said power is inevitable. Tacitus may have also here in mind Tiberius' (disingenuous?) interest in 'harmony' as a concept, reflected in his construction and commemoration on coinage of the Temple of Concord.

certe non adversus habebatur: 'he was considered at least not to be hostile'. A remark seemingly designed to suggest a better moral character to Drusus that that of Sejanus.

vetus et saepe simulatum . . . consilium: 'an old and often simulated plan'. Tacitus himself makes only two references to Tiberius' intention to leave Rome (I.47.1–3, where he is conflicted over the issue, but goes so far as to assemble baggage and load ships [AD 14]); and III.47.2 where, following the campaign against the Aedui, Tiberius espoused interest in heading to Germany [AD 21]).

praetexebat imperator: 'as commander of the armed forces he dissembled'. *praetego* again conveys the sense of deceit and duplicity that characterizes Tiberius' reign in Tacitus' mind. That here Tiberius seems to use the (albeit real) issue of veteran settlement and the recruitment of provincial soldiers as a mere excuse to leave Rome further undercuts the quality of his leadership.

AS

quod mihi quoque exsequendum reor, quae: '... which I think that I too should go through, [namely] what...'. Here **quod** is to be seen as the subject of **exsequendum** and serves to introduce the Indirect Question. Tacitus gives his ensuing summary of the military dispositions, the allied kings, and the extent of the empire for two reasons: 1) a contrast with the situation in his own time; and 2) to highlight the subsequent deterioration under Tiberius himself.

5–6: These chapters serve to illustrate the 'normal' manner of dealing with political business in Rome, with Tacitus including them to serve as a comparison for how they will change for the worse from this point onwards. It is notable that Tacitus here does not blame Tiberius for the paucity of the food supply for the plebs, instead claiming that he dealt with the problem as best he could.

7–12 (AD 23)

These chapters cover the death of Drusus on 14 September, but that event itself is treated cursorily by Tacitus. Rather he chooses to focus on the aftermath, the subsequent meeting of the Senate, and the funeral of Drusus. Tacitus also uses an extended section for an excursus on the contemporary rumours surrounding Drusus' death. The entire approach reinforces Tacitus' primary concerns (see Introduction, pages 14–16).

7.1

quae cuncta: 'all these things'. Refers to the details of chapter 6, where Tiberius' actions relating to the food supply and the administration of the provinces are touched upon; additionally details of Tiberius' personal life and restrained lifestyle are given. The purpose is to contrast with an apparent change in his behaviour subsequent to Drusus' (II) death in AD 23.

AS

non quidem comi via sed horridus ac plerumque formidatus: 'not indeed in a gracious manner, but being severe and often feared'. The *variatio* on **comi via** (Ablative of Manner) with **horridus** and **formidatus** (adj./partic.) serves to emphasize Tacitus condemnation of Tiberius. Even though the latter's actions here are positive, the manner is criticized. **formidatus** again is indicative of the 'climate of fear' under Tiberius that Tacitus wishes to evoke.

nam dum superfuit, mansere: 'for as long as he survived, they remained'. Note the emphatic use of the syncopated perfect **mansere**, essentially repeating the idea from the earlier **retinebat**, to stress that Drusus' (II) death was a turning point in Tiberius' reign.

ultor: 'avenger'. Referring to Drusus (II).

adiutorem imperii: 'assistant of imperial power'. The role which Sejanus had engineered for himself (see above on 2.3).

7.2

quantum superesse ut collega dicatur: 'how small a step remained until he was called colleague?'. Rendered as acc. + infin. as an exclamation in oratio obliqua.

in arduo: 'an uphill task'. Lit. 'in difficulty'; the metaphor of a journey or a climb is continued by **sis ingressus** ('you have entered'), noting the use of the 'ideal' second person (*NLS* §217 note i).

studia: 'sympathies'. *OLD* 5a, 6.

exstructa iam sponte praefecti castra: 'a camp had already been built by the will of the prefect'. See *Annals* IV.2.1. Tacitus makes Sejanus the driving force here.

exstructa ... datos ... cerni: 'built ... given ... seen'. The promotion of the verbs is indicative of the degree and number of Drusus' (II) complaints.

communes ... nepotes: 'his grandsons would be shared ...'. *Annals* III.29.4 speaks of a betrothal between Sejanus' daughter and Drusus (IV), one of Claudius' two children by his first wife, Plautia Urgulanilla. Drusus (IV) died soon after the betrothal. Sejanus' attempts to link his own family with that of the emperor is an effort to acquire legitimacy.

precandam modestiam: 'restraint should be prayed for'. Drusus' appeal to the gods here is suggestive of the limitless ambition of Sejanus, along with the apparent powerlessness of Drusus to intervene.

7.3

neque raro neque apud paucos talia iaciebat: 'Drusus used to toss about such ideas neither infrequently nor in the presence of a few people'. The **litotes** here is hugely emphatic as to the frequency of Drusus' complaints. **iaciebat** is frequently used by Tacitus to discuss the 'tossing out' of hostile comments.

corrupta uxore: 'his corrupted wife'. Could be read as Ablative Absolute, but perhaps more interesting would be to see this as the bare instrumental ablative (*NLS* §44), with the omission of the preposition being typical if the person is regarded as a mere instrument in the hands of another, as indeed Livilla is for Sejanus.

8.1

igitur Seianus maturandum ratus: 'Therefore, Sejanus – thinking that he must hurry – ...'. **igitur** resumes the narrative of 7.1 following the sidebar of Drusus' complaints. The degree of Drusus' (II) hostility also explains why Sejanus now hastens to act.

quo paulatim repente: 'by whose gradual insertion'. The phrase is evocative of the cunning and thought-through nature of the crime. It could also be read as a metaphor for Sejanus' own ascension.

AS

Lygdum spadonem: 'the eunuch Lygdus'. Most likely this individual served as Drusus' (II) praegustator.

octo post annos: 'eight years later'. i.e. in AD 31.

8.2

per omnes . . . dies: 'through all the days'. The clause here is lacking a verb, and the later **ingressus est** is unique in aspect and thus cannot be transposed across directly. However, converting its sense into an imperfect (i.e. *ingrediebatur*) conveys the sense of the clause.

nullo metu an ut firmitudinem animi ostendaret: 'with no fear or in order to show his strength of spirit'. Again the variatio of abl. noun ~ Final (i.e. Purpose) Clause, coordinated by *an*, is typical for Tacitus, reflecting his tendency to provide weighted alternatives.

per speciem maestitiae: 'by the pretext of sorrow'. Again evoking the atmosphere of falsity. It is telling that here Tiberius also sits upon a **sede vulgari** ('common seat'), so we may add hypocrisy to the complaints Tacitus directs at the emperor.

honoris locique: 'place of honour'. Emphatic **hendiadys**.

victo gemitu: 'having conquered his own grief'. Tiberius, as has been typical of his reign, seeks to set an example (see also Suetonius *Tib.* 34 on his 'setting an example against waste').

simul: 'and at the same time'. **simul** here is perhaps best interpreted as coordinating the Ablative Absolute with the inserted **oratione continua**.

oratione continua: 'an unbroken speech'. The speech as recorded, however, is not unbroken: **miseratusque . . . petivit** seems to divide the speech into a section of oratio obliqua and the subsequent section that is rendered as oratio recta.

AS

It must be remembered that speeches in Tacitus, aside from brief quotations, are the construction of the author himself. The speeches would usually vary in style and composition to that of the historian's own narrative, composed to fit the character of the individual as they are presented in the text. This may include elements or mannerisms particular to that individual, or at least be formulated to recall the manner of said individual.

8.3

imbecillitatis: 'for weakness'. Abstract nouns seem to dominate Tiberius speeches and letters (see Miller 1968: 14).

Augustae: The title by which Tiberius' mother, the widow of Augustus, was known after her husband's death (see *Annals* I.8.1). Livia was now 80 years old (born 58 BC) and endured as a significant force at the imperial court until her death in AD 29. Tacitus describes her as 'an unruly mother, a complaisant wife, and a good match for the qualities of her husband and the hypocrisy of her son' (*Annals* V.1.3).

nepotum: 'of his grandsons'. i.e. Nero and Drusus (III).

unica praesentium molrum levamenta: 'he only relief for his present evils'. The **chiastic** arrangement here stresses the force of Tiberius' claims, although Tacitus' phraseology is verging on cliché.

8.4

adulescentulos: 'the boys'. The diminutive form here carries on the imagery from **rudem** ('inexperienced youth') and is picked up again in **deductos** ('escorted'). The presentation of Nero and Drusus (III) is formulated to make them seem helpless and in need of guidance.

orbatos parente: 'bereft of their father'. Germanicus had died in AD 19.

quamquam esset illi propria suboles: 'although he had children of his own'. Most likely referring to Drusus' (II) children, Germanicus and Tiberius Gemellus. The choice of **suboles** is interesting: while its archaic quality befits Tiberius' literary style, it may also reflect the primacy of Drusus' children in terms of succession.

sibique et posteris confirmaret: '... that he should strengthen them, both for myself and for posterity'. While it may be thought that the –*que* suffix links **confirmaret** to the two preceding subjunctives, it is better read as being a 'both ... and' with the ensuing **et**. This allows for a balance with the lack of co-ordination with **suscipite, regite** below.

8.5

disque et patria coram: '... and in the presence of the gods and the fatherland'. Here the suffix –*que* does co-ordinate the two main clauses. Given the way in which Tacitus has previously highlighted the hypocrisy of Tiberius, the strength of his oath here seems somewhat disingenuous.

sucipite, regite: 'take up ... guide'. The asyndeton between these two imperatives has been read as a further example of the Tiberian styling of this speech. *suscipere* is technical for a father acknowledging a child, or is used when a child is adopted into another family.

9.1

impleverat: 'he would have filled'. Pluperfect Indicative in the apodosis of a mixed conditional clause, designed to communicate 'sheer rhetorical exaggeration, whereby what might have happened is vividly presented as fact' (*NLS* §200 (iii)).

totiens: 'so often'. Suetonius (*Div. Aug.* 28.1) tells us that Augustus had 'twice thought of seriously restoring the republic', in 29 and 23 BC. The fact that the two Constitutional Settlements followed these dates in fairly rapid succession (27 and 23 BC, respectively), plus the fact that the Principate had now been Rome's system of government since 27 BC, perhaps accounts for why Tacitus describes these discussions in Tiberius' current speech as **vana et inrisa** ('empty and laughable').

revolutus: 'relapsing' (see *OLD* 4a). The sense of 'relapsing' here takes us back to the opening days of Tiberius' rule, where he made overtures to the Senate for assistance in governing the empire (*Annals* I.11.1; Suetonius *Tib.* 24). At that point in his history, as he does here, Tacitus makes it clear that Tiberius' words are not to be trusted.

9.2

in Germanicum: 'for Germanicus'. Elliptical for *in memoriam Germanici*. *Annals* II.83 records a partial list of the honours that were voted for Germanicus. We also possess the (albeit fragmentary) *Tabula Siarensis* and *Tabula Hebana*, both of which contained an inscription of the *rogatio* (senatorial bill) on the honours for Germanicus. The fact that here Drusus enjoys **plerisque additis** ('very many additional things') is perhaps designed to communicate Tiberius' favour for his natural son over his adopted one.

imaginum pompa: 'a procession of ancestral images'. The presence of ancestral busts in the funeral cortege was a vivid demonstration of the ancestry of the deceased, as well as providing a good example of the constant presence of the past in the present in the Roman mentality.

Iuliae gentis: 'of the Julian family'. Drusus was counted as a member of the *gens Iulia* as a result of Augustus' adoption of Tiberius. This may seem strange to modern eyes, but for the Romans adoption entailed the adoptee legitimately partaking in the history and ancestry of the family. It also accounts for more than a little of the complexity of the average Roman family tree!

Aeneas ... Alborum reges ... Romulus: 'Aeneas ... the kings of the Albans ... Romulus'. This list of the great ancestors of *gens Iulia* is expressive of just how much 'legitimacy' membership of the family afforded its members. The family took its name from Iulus (also known as Ascanius), the son of Aeneas. Thus the new imperial dynasty could claim descent from the originators of the Roman bloodline.

Sabina nobilitas, Attus Clausus ceteraeque Claudiorum effigies: '... the Sabine nobility, Attus Clausus and other images of the Claudians'. The Claudians, i.e. the blood family of Tiberius and Drusus, could themselves claim a healthy heritage at Rome. Suetonius (*Tib.* 1.1) informs us that the patrician branch of the Claudians came from the Sabine town of Regillae, but moved to Rome of the advice of one Atta Claudius (Tacitus' *Attus Clausus*) some six years after the expulsion of the kings, i.e. in 504 BC.

10–11 (AD 23)

These two chapters form a self-contained excursus on the death of Drusus, where Tacitus engages in a lengthy account of the popular rumours surrounding the event. The episode serves several purposes, but perhaps the most significant are: 1) it allows Tacitus the opportunity for proving his own credibility as a historian, as he seemingly investigates and dismisses an outlandish rumour; 2) it allows him to present an entertaining episode to his readers, handled in a way not unlike a rhetorical exercise; and 3) it gives him the opportunity for further character assassination of Tiberius, through the recording of the contemporary opinions on the emperor, while affording himself the defence of 'dismissing a pernicious rumour'. All-in-all, taken as a vignette, the episode serves as a microcosm of the Tacitean approach.

AS

10.1

plurimis maximaeque fidei auctoribus: '... by very many authors of
the greatest reliability'. *variatio* of adjective and descriptive genitive.
The mention of *plurimi auctores* is common in Tacitus and is
necessarily used to suggest reliability, although the degree to which
we are convinced is highly subjective.

eorundem temporum rumorem: 'a rumour of those times'. The fact
that this belief was contemporary supposedly lends it historical
credence. While this may seem odd to us, the concept of 'no smoke
without fire' was a frequent form of evidence even in Roman law-
courts, leaving as it did a lingering doubt in the minds of the jury or,
in this case, in the minds of Tacitus' readers.

validum adeo ut nondum exolescat: '... so strong that it has not yet
faded away'. Thus providing further justification for its inclusion, in
oratio obliqua, in the narrative for AD 23.

10.2

quod ... erat: 'because he was ...'. Tacitus frequently retains the
Indicative Mood in subordinate clauses in Indirect Speech. The effect
it creates is that he is almost 'live-reporting' the rumour.

10.3

tamquam: 'as if'. While this could be read as 'that', providing the
substance of the suspicion, it is perhaps better read as 'as if', which
conveys that this is Tacitus' own explanation of what the suspicion
was.

mortem quam patri struxerat: '... the death which he had contrived
for his father'. The verb has nefarious connotations, and Tacitus often
uses it in the Tiberian hexad for the various political intrigues.

AS

11.1

haec vulgo iactata . . . prompte refutaveris: 'These things, commonly tossed about, . . . one could swiftly refute'. Generalizing second person singular perfect subjunctive in a main clause (*NLS* §119). The verb imparts a decided air of legalese into the speech, adding to the sense that this is somewhat of a rhetorical exercise for the author. However, the flavour of the law-court also makes us imagine Tacitus as flitting between prosecutor and defence attorney in this episode.

quis . . . inaudito filio exitium offeret?: 'Who . . . would have offered destruction to his son unheard?' Imperfect subjunctive for past potential (*NLS* §121). The rhetorical question is very much an authorial comment on Tacitus' part.

tantis rebus exercitus: 'practised in such great matters'. Perhaps an allusion to the maiestas trials.

insita denique etiam in extraneos cunctatione et mora adversum unicum . . . uteretur: '. . . and finally even to use his natural hesitation and delay against strangers towards his only son . . .'. *cunctans* is a frequent description of Tiberius in Tacitus' account of his reign, with the image it creates very much contrasting with the dynamism that had characterized Augustus' reign – indeed it is a most un-statesmanlike quality in the Roman mindset (one need only think of the contemporary disaffection in which Quintus Fabius Maximus Verrucosus was viewed for his 'delaying' tactics against Hannibal). Likewise Suetonius (*Tib.* 21.2) also records an alleged remark of Augustus that he pitied Rome as it was 'doomed to be ground by the slow-moving jaws' of Tiberius. **unicum** here is to be read as a noun, 'only son', as *filius* could easily be understood.

11.2

Seianus facinorum omnium repertor habebatur: '. . . Sejanus was considered the author of all crimes'. **repertor** is a noun deployed against both Tiberius and Sejanus, as Tacitus links the two men linguistically in order to stress their political and ideological affiliations.

caritate in eum Caesaris et ceterorum in utrumque odio: 'out of Caesar's excessive affection for him and the hatred of others for each of them'. This is a beautiful chiasmus which stresses the equal weight on both of the causal ablatives (**caritate**; **odio**).

atrociore semper fama erga dominantium exitus: 'since rumour is always more horrific in the case of the deaths of rulers'. Examples of this phenomenon are extant in the work of various authors, including Tacitus (*Annals* I.5.1) on suspicion towards Livia over Augustus' death; Suetonius (*Claud.* 44–45) on the poisoning of Claudius; and Josephus' extended account of the assassination of Gaius (*Jewish Antiquities* II.37–114), with the grisly variants provided by Dio Cassius (see especially LIX.29.2).

At this point a brief discussion of the alleged poisoning of Drusus is perhaps warranted. Although Tacitus treats it as fact, it is by no means a clear picture. Here he claims that Sejanus' divorced wife, Apicata, betrayed Sejanus' plot (in AD 30/31), but gives no explanation of how she would have known of it, given that Sejanus had left her prior to the alleged event taking place. Similarly, as Eudemus and Lygdamus were tortured to elicit their evidence (**tormentis Eudemi ac Lygdi patefactus est**), this is hardly reliable testimony. Dio (LVII.14.9–10) describes Drusus as being both violent and a drunkard, suggesting a less-than-temperate lifestyle; while Tacitus himself (*Annals* III.49.1) intimates that Drusus had suffered a serious illness in AD 21. Given that we have already seen that the alleged poisoning resembled a 'natural illness' (8.1: **fortuitus morbus**), the evidence for a poisoning is rather circumstantial. The episode is therefore perhaps more symptomatic of the obfuscation, suspicion, and secrecy that dominates Tacitus' account of Tiberius reign than it is convincing evidence of murderous political intrigues.

11.3

rumoris: 'the rumour'. The repeat of this noun from 10.1 marks the ending of the excursus and creates a pleasing ring composition.

falsas auditiones: 'false hearsays'. Adds stress to the fact that the contents of this particular rumour are beyond belief – not that rumours are in themselves unreliable testimony.

<ne> divulgata atque incredibilia ... antehabeant: '... that they should not prefer gossip and fantasies'. The final observation of Tacitus here is that by reading his history his audience should prefer uncorrupted true accounts (**veris neque in miraculum corruptis**) to baseless gossip and fantastical rumour. There is perhaps a snobbish tone here, but it justifies his long excursus in 'dismissing' the rumour of Tiberius' complicity in the death of his son.

12.1

ceterum: 'Meanwhile'. Resumes the narrative from 9.2.

laudante filium pro rostris Tiberio: '... with Tiberius praising his son from the Rostra'. The Rostra was the public speaking platform in the Forum. Although the site of great public declamations, the Rostra also had come under 'abuse' in the reign of Augustus, being alleged to be the site of his daughter Julia's sexual infidelities (see Dio LV.10.12; Sen. *De ben.* VI.32; Pliny the Elder. *NH* VII.46). However, here there is a sense of solemnity to the oration given by Tiberius on behalf of his son. It should also be noted that there is a distinct contrast here with the treatment which Germanicus received, as he was not 'praised from the Rostra' (*Annals* III.5.1).

habitum ac voces dolentum simulatione magis quam libens induebat: '... putting on the manner and voices of mourners, more in pretence than willingly'. The assertion here is very clear, heightened by discrete pieces of vocabulary that speak towards falsity: *simulatio* is fairly obvious; *induo* almost suggests the wearing of theatrical costume, adding to the overall dramatic presentation of Book IV. Note the Imperfect tense, which conjures the idea that this demeanour was adopted while Tiberius himself was speaking. However, it could also be treated as a Conative Imperfect, i.e. 'they were trying to put on': this would stress the forced nature of their behaviour, and the fact that their mourning was far from heartfelt.

occulti laetabantur: 'they were secretly rejoicing'. **occulti** is in contrast to **induebat** above and again evokes the shadowplay behind the façade that dominates Tacitus' treatment of Tiberian society. The overall effect is one of mistrust and secrecy.

12.2

ferox scelerum: 'exulting in his crimes'. **scelerum** = Objective Genitive, but verges on Genitive of Characteristic. The assessment of Sejanus here is particularly damning, suggesting that his criminality is innate.

neque spargi venenum in tres poterat: 'Nor could he distribute poison against the three of them …'. A nice double meaning on **spargi venenum** here in that it could be taken literally, i.e. even Sejanus could not poison that many people secretly, and metaphorically, i.e. 'to disseminate poison[ous allegations]' in the form of damage to reputation.

pudicitia Agrippinae impenetrabili: 'the impenetrable modesty of Agrippina'. The imagery here is not sexual, but does serve to contrast the moral uprightness of Agrippina with the corruptible quality of Livilla.

contumaciam: 'stubbornness'. Agrippina certainly had the quality of entrenched beliefs and behaviours. Indeed, on his deathbed Germanicus urged his wife to 'cast aside her defiance, to submit her spirit to the savagery of fortune and not … to goad her superiors in power …' (*Annals* II.72.1).

inhiare dominationi: 'that she coveted absolute power'. The imagery here is very evocative. *inhio* conjures images of two tropes: that of a hungry animal gaping for sustenance – certainly ironic when the phrase is put in the mouth of Sejanus; and also that of Tantalus striving for something that is eternally out-of-reach.

Iulium Postumum: 'Julius Postumus'. Possibly the Prefect of Egypt we know of from AD 47 – if so, he must have survived the purge that ensued following Sejanus' fall.

Mutiliae Priscae: 'Mutilia Prisca'. The wife of C. Fufius Geminus (consul AD 29). Dio (LVII.4.6) records that in AD 30 she committed suicide in the Senate chamber by stabbing herself. Her husband, accused of maiestas, had took his own life at the same time.

proximi inliciebantur … tumidos spiritus perstimulare: 'those closest [to Agrippina] were also enticed into inciting her proud spirits'. **tumidos** here echoes and expands on **contumaciam** above. Again, the adjective has certain animalistic undertones (see *OLD* 5a).

13–16: Here Tacitus follows a traditional pattern of Roman history, ending his account of AD 23 with miscellaneous items from the domestic political situation. The entire section seems to serve primarily as a means of delaying the account of the machinations of Sejanus, seemingly as a means of building suspense, but also perhaps to reinforce the fact that all of Sejanus' activities play out in the shadows, behind the façade of seemingly normal senatorial activity.

17–33: (AD 24) These chapters cover much of the material for AD 24, following a familiar tripartite structure of home affairs, foreign affairs, home affairs. Chapter 17 sees the introduction of Tiberius' hostility to the sons of Germanicus, as he lambasts the priests for offering vows for their preservation. The subsequent chapters (18–22) cover Tiberius' actions against supporters of Agrippina and Germanicus, such as C. Silius and Titius Sabinus. Chapter 21 focusses on the accusations against Calpurnius Piso for having private conversations wherein he spoke against Tiberius' sovereignty. With this example, we see the beginnings of a focus upon the suppression of free-speech and the creation of something of a police state, both occurrences that very much irk Tacitus.

Chapters 23–26 cover the account of the conclusion of the protracted campaign against the Numidian Tacfarinas, finally brought to an end by Publius Cornelius Dolabella.

Chapters 27–31 return us to political affairs in Rome, primarily with a lengthy description of the trial of the elder Vibius Serenus, who had been accused by his own son. This example of the transgression of the Roman virtue of pietas serves to illustrate the moral corruption which Tacitus perceives in Rome under Tiberius and Sejanus, speaking towards the breakdown of society.

Chapters 32–33 are a digression from Tacitus on the subject of writing history, and serves to separate the account of AD 24 from that of AD 25. In this striking section Tacitus points out the difference between the periods of history which he is recording compared with the Republican period. He notes that the latter was dominated by 'localities of peoples, fluctuations of battles, and the fates of brilliant leaders' all of which he claims serve to 'rivet and reinvigorate the readers' minds' (33.3). However, he states that his own history is dominated by 'savage orders, constant accusations, deceitful friendships, the ruin of innocents' (ibid.). The digression therefore also serves to bring to the fore the elements that will dominate the coming chapters and Books, beginning in 34–36 with the trial of the historian Cremutius Cordus and continuing in 37–38 with the hypocritical 'false modesty' of Tiberius in rejecting cult worship.

AS

39–41 (AD 25)

Chapters 39–41 comprise the central unit of the narrative of AD 25 and are emblematic of Tacitus' presentation of the relationship between Tiberius and Sejanus. Here Sejanus formally entreats Tiberius for the hand of Livilla in marriage and, when he is forestalled in that hope, he successfully persuades Tiberius to leave Rome. The emperor's departure from the capital of the empire allowed Sejanus to enjoy political supremacy for the next five years.

The episode is presented in the form of an exchange of letters, which may be compared to the delivery of paired speeches. However, as with speeches there is obviously a question as to their authenticity as Tacitus presents them. That being said, certainly in Tiberius' 'letter' there are archaisms and a style of phraseology that is seemingly designed to at least evoke the sense of the emperor's idiolects.

Tacitus is also certainly having a degree of fun in playing with the form of the letter in these chapters. These evidently private letters are of a decidedly public style; in particular that of Sejanus. Letters of recommendation, as Sejanus' may be seen to be, were usually public documents. However, here Tacitus uses this dichotomy of form and content to highlight Sejanus' ambition: this is a *private* letter for *self*-advancement.

Similarly, given Tacitus' secondary nature – and his annalistic form – it would be incredulous to suppose that in his record of this 'letter' from AD 25, he was not also looking to foreshadow the letter of AD 31 that would bring an end to Sejanus' political supremacy. This internal coherence and consistency to the *Annals* is one of the features that makes it such a compelling history of the Julio-Claudian period.

39.1

nimia fortuna socors . . . cupidine incensus: 'careless in his excessive good fortune . . . enflamed by desire'. These two characteristics seem designed to evoke the sense of tragic drama. The hubris of Sejanus will cause his downfall. This hamartia is in keeping with the theatrical themes of Book IV.

muliebri: 'a / the woman's' (adj.). While the adjective can also mean 'for the woman', this interpretation does not fit well with the pretended affection that Sejanus demonstrated (see 3.3). Rather, as the ensuing phrase would emphasize, Livilla now seems to be urging on Sejanus.

quamquam praesentem: 'although he was present [in Rome]'. The phrase perhaps explains what could otherwise be an odd authorial parenthesis. It succeeds not only in foreshadowing Tiberius' later absence from the city, when letters would be necessary to communicate with the emperor (see 67.1), but also in suggesting the reticence of Tiberius to engage personally.

39.2

benevolentia patris Augusti: 'by the kindness of his father Augustus'. Sejanus is here engaging in the practice of captatio benevolentiae. As Augustus was not actually Tiberius' father, the appeal is to that of political precedent.

iudiciis: 'marks of esteem'. *OLD* 10a.

excubias ac labores, ut unum e militibus . . . malle: 'he preferred sentry work and toils, as one of the soldiers'. As Tacitus has gone to great lengths to show the uniqueness of Sejanus' position, such a claim here that he is simply a common soldier is strikingly disingenuous. Tacitus highlights this further through the use of **ut**, which adds ambiguity, being translatable as 'as' or 'as if'.

AS

quod pulcherrimum (sc. *esset*): 'that which was finest'. To be read as the object of **adeptum**, with the following phrase (**ut . . . crederetur**) explaining what is being referred to.

coniunctione Caesaris: 'connection by marriage to Caesar'. See above on 7.2.

39.3

sola necessitudinis gloria usurum: 'who would only enjoy the glory of the relationship'. The sycophantic tone of Sejanus' letter is in keeping with Tacitus' overall presentation of the man. The deceptive nature of Sejanus and the climate of mistrust under Tiberius are both key tropes of the Tiberian hexad.

39.4

non enim exuere imposita munia: 'for he was not laying aside the duties imposed on him'. This rather litotic phrase is precisely the opposite of what Sejanus wishes.

40.1

pietate Seiani: 'the piety of Sejanus'. A remark that verges on the sarcastic: Sejanus is impious throughout the *Annals*, so this is obvious to the reader. It is curious as to whether this *is* dramatic irony, for the remainder of the letter would seem to suggest that Tiberius is fully aware of the disingenuousness of Sejanus.

tamquam ad integram consultationem: 'as though for a full deliberation'. Tiberius' reply is delivered in the same terms with which Sejanus approached him (**consultavisse** at 39.3). The phrase is designed to keep Sejanus on tenterhooks; despite the length of the letter, there is potential for further debate.

ceteris mortalibus: 'other people'. *mortales* for *homines* is an archaism, but one that seems to be designed to deliberately allude to Tiberius' style of rhetoric.

AS

ad famam derigenda: 'to be regulated in light of public opinion'.

40.2

rescriptu: 'in reply'. *rescribere* is the technical term for an imperial response (*OLD* 2a). The use of the term here is perhaps marking a boundary between Tiberius as emperor and as a potential father-in-law.

nubendum ... an ... in penatibus iisdem tolerandum haberet: 'whether she should marry ... or continue in the same household'. *habeo* + Gerund(ive) has the sense of 'I have (to do something)'.

post Drusum (sc. *mortuum*): 'after Drusus' (death)'. A typical example of brachylogy.

matrem et aviam: 'her mother and grandmother'. Respectively: Antonia Minor, the widow of Drusus (I) and younger daughter of Marc Antony; and Livia Augusta.

40.3

simplicius acturum: 'he would act more directly'. While the adverb seemingly relates to Tiberius' reply, Tacitus is doubtless alluding to the typical equivocation of Tiberius.

sic quoque: 'even as things were'.

eaque discordia nepotes suos convelli: 'and his grandsons were being torn apart by that strife'. These were Nero and Drusus (III), plus perhaps their brother Gaius (the future emperor). As Tiberius Gemellus was yet an infant, he is unlikely to be being alluded to here.

quid si intendatur certamen tali coniugio?: 'what if the quarrel were intensified by such a marriage?'. Tiberius argues that the cohesiveness of the imperial family is of prime importance to him. There is an irony here in that his treatment of Germanicus and Agrippina has heightened the factionalism (see *Annals* II.1–6.3).

AS

40.4

falleris enim, Seiane: 'For you are deceived, Sejanus . . .'. The transition into direct speech is quite effective in adding emotion to the argument as Tiberius outlines his position. The verb *fallo* should also be noted.

C. Caesar: 'Gaius Caesar'. The son of Julia, daughter of Augustus, and Marcus Agrippa. He had died in AD 4.

fratrem . . . patrem . . . maiores nostros: 'brother . . . father . . . our ancestors'. The tricolon is effective in communicating Tiberius' mistrust of public sentiment. That *Annals* VI.46.2 records '. . . his concern was not so much contemporaries' goodwill as popularity among posterity', leads us to question the honesty of Tiberius' statement here.

40.5

qui te invitum perrumpunt omnibusque de rebus consulunt: 'who intrude upon you against your wishes and consult you on all matters'. In IV.2.3 Tacitus alleges that Sejanus had been making a conscious effort to ingratiate himself with the Senate, thus making this remark ironic. *perrumpo* is used metaphorically here, as elsewhere in the Tiberian hexad, perhaps suggesting an idiolect of the emperor.

excessisse iam pridem equestre fastigium: 'that you have long since exceeded the pinnacle of an *eques*'. Sejanus' great power (see above on chapter 2) and his relatively humble background (1.2) were a source of criticism, especially in Tacitus' eyes. The more pro-Tiberian Velleius Paterculus attempts to counter these facets of Sejanus' unpopularity in II.127–28.

amicitias: 'friendships'. The term is decidedly pointed, designed to evoke the relationship between Augustus and Maecenas. Maecenas had been Augustus' great colleague and deputy, acting very much on the socio-cultural side of Augustus' regime, for example as the patron of the poet Horace (*Odes* I.1.1–2). Seneca (*On Benefits* VI.32.2–4) testifies to the service that Maecenas provided to the first Emperor. Here Tiberius seems to be suggesting that Sejanus has already exceeded the limits of this previous 'friendship'.

40.6

mirum hercule si, cum . . .: 'What a surprise that, when . . .'. An ironic remark, where the opposite is intended.

nullis rei publicae negotiis permixtos: 'mixed up in none of the business of the state'. That Augustus considered such men is in no way a surprise given his desire to retain power within his own bloodline. Proculeius (see below) was certainly *not* one of these figures.

C. Proculeium: A Roman eques and a close acquaintance of Augustus, even prior to Actium. Dio (LIV.3) claims that Proculeius was a brother of the Murena condemned in 22 BC for conspiring against Augustus. However, Dio also comments on the intimacy between Proculeius and Augustus (ibid.), placing him at the same level as Maecenas.

sed si dubitatione Augusti movemur: 'But if we are moved by the hesitation of Augustus . . .'. Tiberius reverses Sejanus' use of Augustus as a trump card. The use of the 'Royal We' (**movemur**) also reinforces Tiberius' superiority.

quanto validius est quod: 'how much more telling it is that . . .'. Ultimately, Augustus did *not* betroth Julia to an eques of little political impact. In 21 BC Julia was married to Marcus Agrippa. Upon his death in 12 BC, she married Tiberius in the following year.

40.7

non occultavi: 'I have not concealed'. Completes the sense of the section begun by **simplicius acturum**. However, once again the reader is forced to bring to mind the secrecy and deceit that have dominated the Book.

AS

ceterum neque tuis neque Liviae destinatis adversabor: 'I shall not oppose your plans nor those of Livilla'. This remark comes as something of a surprise given the preceding arguments, but it again fits with the double-dealing and duplicity of the Tiberian regime as Tacitus has presented it.

omittam ad praesens referre: 'I shall refrain from mentioning for the present', This phraseology, designed to keep Sejanus hanging on, is representative of the *suspensa semper et obscura verba* (I.11.2) for which Tiberius has been renowned.

quibus adhuc necessitudinibus immiscere te mihi parem: 'with what further bonds I am preparing to link you to me'. The phrase presents some issues from the historical perspective, as it calls into question how Sejanus' relationship with the imperial family developed. Suetonius (*Tib.* 65.1) describes him as *spe adfinitatis … deceptum* ('deceived by the hope of alliance by marriage'); but Dio (LVIII.7.5) refers to him as 'betrothed' to someone, but fails to provide an identity for this individual; Tacitus himself refers to Sejanus later in the *Annals* as Tiberius' son-in-law. It is possible that Sejanus did indeed marry Livilla at some point prior to AD 31, but the situation is unclear.

vel in senatu vel in contione non reticebo: 'either in the Senate of in the Assembly, I shall not keep quiet'. The phrase fits the context of the letter by indicating that Tiberius will (at some point) publicly announce the betrothal for which Sejanus hopes. However, it also foreshadows 18 October AD 31, where Sejanus is denounced in front of the Senate.

41.1

rursum Seianus non iam de matrimonio: 'In reply, Sejanus no longer [argued] about the marriage'. The immediacy of the remark highlights the rapidity of Sejanus' response, but also how he must now change tack.

altius metuens: 'fearing more deeply'. The comparative adverb here is perhaps suggestive of the anxiety that Sejanus usually feels. Given his own political machinations, his suspicion of others is entirely understandable.

tacita suspicionum, vulgi rumorem, ingruentam invidiam: 'the silences of the suspicious, the envy of the common people, the increasing envy'. The tricolon and asyndeton both contribute to the desperate quality of Sejanus' reply.

ut Tiberium ad vitam procul Roma amoenis locis degendam impelleret: 'to compel Tiberius to live his life far from Rome in attractive places'. Sejanus' choice is either to step away from power himself or to manipulate the emperor to serve his own ends. This new plan adds not only to Sejanus' over-arching ambition, but also will highlight the selfishness of Tiberius. **procul** stresses the distance that Tiberius will be from the political centre; **amoenis** is the typical adjective applied to attractive places.

41.2

secretoque loci mollitum: 'softened by the seclusion of the place'. This is Sejanus' secret hope for the sending away of Tiberius. Also note the common Tacitean *variatio* on the Ablative Absolute **vergente senecta** and the participle **mollitum**.

minui ... augeri: 'would be reduced ... would be augmented'. The chiastic arrangement (infinitive – abl. absol. – abl. absol. – infinitive) serves to emphasize the antithesis between these two verbs.

41.3

negotia urbis, populi adcursus, multitudinem adfluentium: 'the business of the city, the hasty arrival of the people, the host of those flooding in'. The tricolon adds emphasis to Sejanus' condemnation of life at Rome.

increpat, extollens laudibus: '... he rebuked, while extolling with praises ...'. The standard oratorical antithesis between blame and praise is highlighted by the **juxtaposition** of the verbs.

quis abesse taedia et offensiones ac praecipua rerum maxime agitari: 'from which weariness and resentment were absent and in which the most important of affairs could be especially considered'. **quis** is an archaic form for *quibus*, which Tacitus prefers in the *Annals*. It stands as Ablative of Separation with **abesse**, and as Local Ablative with **agitari**. Sejanus here once again demonstrates his cunning; the contrast between **offensiones** and **praecipua rerum** adds to the persuasiveness of his argument.

42–44: *These chapters summarize the end of* AD *25, again focussing in on senatorial business. The catalogue is used as further motivation for Tiberius to depart from Rome as a result of the 'generally true and serious utterances which were thrust at him when he was present' (42.1).*

45: *This chapter discusses the death of the praetor Lucius Piso in Spain, when he is ambushed by 'a certain rustic of the Termestine nation' (45.1). Again the chapter is perhaps best seen as being transitional, passing from the obituaries in 44 into the insurrection of 46. However, we may also be being manipulated to see this 'frightful act' as indicative of 'barbarian' peoples, as Tacitus so presents it. Thus when Romans, i.e. Sejanus and Tiberius, go on to perform such atrocities in subsequent chapters, their behaviour is necessarily also to be classified as 'barbaric', i.e. non-Roman.*

46–51: *The chapters cover the insurrection in Thrace, although its placement in the account at the beginning of* AD *26 is ahistorical, given that it was concluded in the second half of the year (51.3). The fact that chapter 52 opens with the focus on the disruption caused by purely domestic political events is perhaps designed to reinforce that the wider empire was of little significance to those in power.*

52–54 (AD 26)

These chapters are concerned with the relationship between Tiberius and Agrippina, the widow of Germanicus, and serves as a companion piece to chapters 39–41. The contents elucidate the various lines of attack which Sejanus has set in motion, as well as illustrating the characters of the various players. The relationship between Agrippina and Tiberius is a complex (though largely acrimonious) one. Various authors (such as Suetonius, *Tib.* 53 and 64) use it as a vignette for the cruelties of Tiberius, although Velleius Paterculus (*History of Rome*

A
Level

II.130.4), in a moment typical of his pro-Principate stance, speaks of the 'sorrow, the fury, the shame [Tiberius] was compelled to endure because of his daughter-in-law, Agrippina'.

52.1

at Romae commota principis domo: 'But at Rome, with the household of the princeps shaken ...'. Following the interlude of 43–51, which have dealt with foreign affairs, **at Romae** is a conventional transition back into the sphere of domestic politics. The source of the upheaval has been much discussed, with some arguing for the death of Drusus (8.1ff.), others the machinations of Sejanus (12.2–4), while yet others the letters of Sejanus and Tiberius, plus the latter's subsequent departure from Rome (39–41). Given the turbulence of Book IV, a confluence of all of the events is not beyond possibility, but the last in the sequence is certainly the most pointed and precise.

ut series futuri in Agrippinam exitii inciperet: 'so that the process of future destruction for Agrippina could begin'. **in** + acc. is common in pointing out a potential victim. The phrase also communicates the cunning of Sejanus, the well thought-through nature of his plans, and the gradual escalation of his daring.

Claudia Pulchra: 'Claudia Pulchra'. Agrippina's second cousin – the daughter of Augustus' niece Marcella minor. She was also the widow of Quin(c)tilius Varus, the commander who lost three legions in the Teutoburg Forest in AD 9 (see Suetonius *Div. Aug.* 23).

Domitio Afro: 'Domitius Afer'. Gnaeus Domitius Afer was an outstanding Roman orator, who became suffect consul in AD 39; he died in AD 59. His description as **quoquo facinore properus clarescere** ('quick to shine, whatever the deed') perhaps says much about the flexibility and lack of scruple needed to be a successful politician under the Principate. Dio (LIX.19) records that in a

A
Level

subsequent encounter with Agrippina, Afer stepped aside from her path 'out of embarrassment (for his prosecution of Claudia Pulchra)', whereupon Agrippina remarked: 'Fear not, Domitius; it isn't you that I hold to blame, but Agamemnon.' Domitius Afer also suffered an attempt at prosecution by the emperor Gaius (ostensibly motivated in part by the same prosecution of Claudia Pulchra [ibid.]) only escaping execution by grovelling to the emperor, which pleased Gaius no end. Domitius Afer's career thus reveals much about the political vagaries of the period.

crimen impudicitiae, adulterum Furnium: 'a charge of immorality, with Furnius as her lover'. Furnius himself is otherwise unknown, but the charge of immorality is one that was often deployed against imperial women.

veneficia in principem devotiones: 'poisonings and curses directed at the princeps'. These were standard accusations in cases of maiestas (see Introduction, page 3).

obiectabat: 'he flung out'. The verb could be treated to communicate not only the somewhat circumstantial and unconvincing nature of the accusations, but also ferocity of the prosecution instigated by Sejanus.

52.2

semper atrox: 'always fiery'. **atrox** here again speaks towards the temperament of Agrippina (see 12.2).

non in effigies mutas divinum spiritum transfusum: 'his divine spirit had not passed across into mute likenesses'. A particularly affecting remark. Here Agrippina begins her assertion of her blood relationship to Augustus, mirrored in that she also resembled him in temperament. **transfusum** calls to mind metempsychosis, or the transmigration of the soul.

A
Level

se imaginem veram, caelesti sanguinem ortam: 'she was his true likeness, she the offspring of his heavenly blood'. The tone of accusation towards Tiberius here is unmistakeable; as a mere adoptee, he is merely a pretender to the line of Augustus.

intellegere discrimen, suscipere sordes: 'she understood the crisis [and] was adopting sack-cloth'. The Indirect Speech makes it clear that this is still reporting Agrippina's actual words to Tiberius. The former clause reveals her political astuteness; the latter the inevitable outcome of Claudia Pulchra's trial. **sordes** refers to the dark clothing worn both by mourners and also by defendants in court. Agrippina's remark thus also reinforces that she fully understands that her own prosecution will follow hard upon that of Claudia Pulchra. Note the insidious sibilance on **suscipere sordes**.

frustra Pulchram praescribi: 'It was pointless that Pulchra was used as a pretext'. The execution of Pulchra could serve as nothing else than a precursor to the prosecution of Agrippina herself.

cui sola exitii causa sit quod Agrippinam stulte prorus ad cultum delegerit: 'the sole reason for whose destruction was that she had stupidly chosen Agrippina as the object of her affection.' The phrase has a certain pathetic quality to it, characterizing Pulchra as a hapless victim of circumstances beyond her ken. Agrippina's referring to herself in the Third Person (**Agrippinam**) is also pathetic, but has the added advantage of adding a note of haughtiness in keeping with the tone of the preceding clauses.

oblita Sosiae ob eadem adflictae: 'forgetting that Sosia had been dealt with in the same way'. This refers to Sosia Galla, the wife of Gaius Silius. Silius had been a friend of Germanicus, who had also been prosecuted at Sejanus' instigation (*Annals* IV.18.1–19.4). While her husband had committed suicide to 'pre-empt his looming destruction', Sosia herself was exiled (IV.20.2).

52.3

audita haec raram occulti pectoris vocem elicuere: 'Hearing these things elicited a rare remark from that secretive breast'. **elicuere** is a syncopated Third Person Plural, from the Neuter Plural **haec** as subject. Once again the typical reticence and secrecy of Tiberius is highlighted (cf. Annals I.11.2: 'Tiberius' words, even on matters where he was not concealing, were – whether by nature or habit – always weighed and dark').

correptamque: A questionable reading of the MSS, as *arremptamque* could be more suitable. The sense is 'and grabbed her by the hand' if **correptamque** is correct. Suetonius (*Tib*. 53.1) in reporting the same moment states: *liberius quiddam questam manu apprehendit* ('he took her by the hand when she had complained a little too liberally').

Graeco versu admonuit: 'he admonished her with a Greek verse'. Again Suetonius quotes the alleged remark: *'Si non dominaris,' inquit, 'filiola, iniuriam te accipere existimas?'* ('If you are not queen, my dear,' he said, 'do you think that you have received some injury?'). Tiberius certainly seems to have a penchant for aphorisms in Greek, sometimes using them as a means of catching out certain 'experts' (Suetonius *Tib*. 70).

prosperiore eloquentiae quam morum fama fuit: 'his reputation was more favourable for his eloquence than for his morality'. See above on Domitius Afer's subsequent career.

retinet silentii impatientiam: 'he retained his inability to endure silence'. This does not exactly tally with the report given in Dio (LIX.19.4).

53.1

pervicax irae et morbo corporis implicata: 'persisting in her anger and gripped by a physical disease'. The stubbornness of Agrippina is now even more marked, despite her physical frailty.

A
Level

habilem adhuc iuventam sibi: 'she was still suitably youthful'. Agrippina was born in 15 BC, meaning that she was now 41 years old. Her remark is therefore somewhat a stretch; the reality of the situation is also affected by **morbo corporis implicata** above.

neque aliud probis quam ex matrimonio solacium: 'nor is there any solace for the virtuous save that from marriage'. Agrippina's remarking of herself as *proba*, plus the pointed comment on marriage to the unwed Tiberius, would be unlikely to effect her success.

esse in civitate ***: 'there are in the community [those men] ***'. The break in the manuscript here is problematic. It could be easily solved by the insertion of the Relative Pronoun (Masc. Nom. Pl.) *qui*, to immediately connect to the verb **dignarentur**. However, the text break seems to be significantly longer than that which could be covered by this single word.

53.2

non ignarus quantum ex re publica peteretur: 'not unaware of how much was demanded by the state' (**ex** = 'on the part of'). The Latin here is complicated as there are two equally convincing and appropriate translations, both revolving around the interpretation of **peteretur**. The first would be inferring *ab Agrippina* with the verb, i.e. 'he was not unaware of how much was being demanded from the state [by Agrippina]'. This translation has the advantage of communicating the political awareness of Tiberius, that although Agrippina's request for a husband is personal it has political implications resulting from her being related to Augustus. The second interpretation (that preferred here), is that **peteretur** be taken without a definite person implied. This translation has the advantage of tying in with Tiberius' own unwilling acceptance of the responsibilities of the Principate, the subordinating of personal desires for the good of the state.

A
Level

ne tamen offensionis aut metus manifestus foret: 'however, so as there would be no trace of affront or fear …'. **tamen** here contrasts with **non ignarus quantum ex re publica peteretur** which necessarily implies a refusal on Tiberius' part to allow Agrippina to re-marry. **metus** most likely refers to his concerns over the possibility of the fortunes of Germanicus' family improving.

id ego, a scriptoribus annalium non traditum, repperi in commentariis Agrippinae filiae: 'this, not transmitted by the writers of histories, *I* uncovered in the records of Agrippina's daughter'. Once again Tacitus takes the opportunity to celebrate his own powers of research, while at the same time denigrating the work of his predecessors. Agrippina the Younger, daughter of Germanicus and Agrippina the Elder, was born in AD 15 and was murdered by her son, the emperor Nero, in AD 59.

casus suorum posteris memoravit: 'she recalled for posterity the deaths of her family'. **casus suorum** refers to the fates of her mother and her two brothers, Nero and Drusus (III), which all occurred between AD 31–33.

54.1

ceterum Seianus maerentem et improvidam altius perculit: 'Yet Sejanus struck the grieving and misguided woman more deeply'. **ceterum** again resumes the narrative after the note about Agrippina the Younger's records. It is noteworthy that the tactics that Sejanus employs against Agrippina (**monerent paratum ei venenum**: 'who would warn her that poison had been prepared for her'), are very similar to those dismissed in the rumour in 10.2–3.

immissis: 'sending in people'. Sejanus' plots frequently involve secondary parties, ensuring that he has the defence of plausible deniability.

A
Level

per speciem amicitiae: 'under the appearance of friendship'. **speciem** once again conjures the theme of deceit and falsity that dominates these chapters. *amicitia* is more than simple 'friendship', rather being the relationship that served as the socio-political glue of the Roman world. Its abuse under Tiberius' reign is a key theme for Tacitus that speaks towards the topsy-turvy morality of the period.

simulationum nescia: 'unaware of [Sejanus'] deceptions'. This is perhaps the preferred translation to alternatives such as 'unable to put on an act'. The preferred translation has the advantage of characterizing Agrippina as of a more 'Roman' attitude than Sejanus and Tiberius.

poma ... laudans nurui sua manu tradidit: 'praising an apple, he passed it to his daughter-in-law with his own hand'. This entire dinner party episode plays somewhat like a melodrama, and that is surely the effect for which Tacitus aimed. *nurus*, as with *socer* ('father-in-law') above create a markedly domestic image, which has been corrupted by the intrigues of Sejanus.

54.2

obversus ad matrem: 'turning to his mother'. Livia Augusta, who had a deep-seated hostility towards Agrippina (see 12.3).

a qua veneficii insimularetur: 'by whom he was being incriminated for poisoning'. The simple remark confirms the effectiveness of Sejanus' machinations.

inde rumor parari exitium: 'Thence a rumour that her destruction was being prepared'. Once again rumour takes hold in a society plagued by secrecy and mistrust; the degree of obfuscation is heightened by **secretum** in the next clause, which has the sense of 'with no witnesses'.

55–56: This brief discussion of senatorial business, focussing on a temple for Tiberius in the province of Asia, serves as little more than an example of the type of business that Tiberius is using to 'deflect' the rumours that he was plotting the death of Agrippina.

A
Level

57–60 (AD 26)

This section covers the departure of Tiberius from Rome to Campania, and thence to Capri. This event is perhaps the most significant in the Tiberian period, but in Tacitus' account it is rather the way in which his departure is exploited by Sejanus that takes centre stage.

The theatricality of Book IV continues in this section, with Sejanus once again cast in the mould of master-manipulator, setting the scenes and casting the various roles that will allow him to become the most influential figure in the empire until his eventual downfall in AD 31.

57.1

inter quae: 'meanwhile'. The phrase is designed to suggest that Tiberius' departure from Rome almost interrupts the senatorial debate that was taking place at 55.1. Thus the suddenness and unexpected nature of the departure, from the perspective of everyone save Tiberius and Sejanus, is stressed.

diu meditato prolatoque saepius consilio: 'having contemplated the plan for a long time and put it off frequently'. This remark is curious as, although it tallies with a comment on his trip to Campania in AD 21 (III.31.2) where he 'gave consideration to a long and continuous absence', it does not accord with the influence of Sejanus which seems to have started only in the previous year (see above on 41).

in Campania <concessit>, specie dedicandi templa: 'he withdrew to Campania, on the pretext of dedicating temples'. The verb *concessit* is supplied to make sense of this vital moment. Indeed the significance of the event makes the deliberate omission of a verb highly unlikely. *concessit* is supplied on the use of this verb in the similar context of III.31.2. **specie** again features as a key piece of vocabulary, calling to mind the falsity of Tiberius' excuse.

A
Level

apud Nolam Augusto: 'and to Augustus at Nola'. Augustus had died at
Nola on 19 August AD 14. The fact that Tiberius is willing to use this
as the pretext (**specie**) of his visit to the region smacks of the impiety
that Tacitus uses here for further denigration of the princeps.

quamquam secutus plurimos auctorum ad Seiani artes rettuli:
'although I have followed the majority of authors and ascribed it to
the skills of Sejanus'. Again this clause requires some analysis of the
context. It would seem to imply that Tacitus' opinion has been that
Sejanus was the primary influence on Tiberius' departure, but this is
not consistent with **diu meditato** etc. above. However, we could see
this as an involved way of setting up a double condemnation of both
Sejanus *and* Tiberius. We have already seen, at 10.1, Tacitus making an
excursus on what he overtly states to be a false rumour. Here he has
the added advantage of the two alternatives not being mutually
exclusive. **artes** again connotes the manipulative expertise of Sejanus;
plurimos auctorum provides an additional layer of condemnation as
Tacitus contextualizes his own critique.

sex postea annos pari secreto coniunxit: 'he continued for six years
afterwards in the same isolation'. i.e. AD 31–37.

plerumque permoveor num ad ipsum referri veritus sit: 'I have
often been moved [to consider] whether it might be more truthful to
ascribe it to the man [i.e. Tiberius] himself'. Tacitus is perhaps
engaging in *reprehensio*, of self-correction, but this is hardly
recrimination; rather it allows him to engage in a lengthy and vivid
treatment of alternative motivations for Tiberius' self-imposed exile,
whilst never formally dismissing the machinations of Sejanus.

saevitiam ac libidinem: 'his savagery and lust'. A full – if gossip-
driven – account of such activities is given by Suetonius (*Tib*. 41–44).
Yet Velleius Paterculus (II.126.4) states that 'our best of emperors is
teaching his citizens by example to do what is right'. The physical

A
Level

separation of emperor and centre of traditional government undoubtedly gave rise to manifold rumours and exaggerations.

57.2

erant qui crederent in senectute corporis quoque habitum pudori fuisse: 'There were those who believed that in his old age the appearance of his body had also been a source of embarrassment'. This remark, simple enough in itself, has caused some debate by virtue of its relationship to the preceding and succeeding clauses. We may be best served in seeing the ensuing **quippe ... interstincta** as parenthetic, allowing **erant ... fuisse** to serve as a foil for **et Rhodi ... insuerat**, thus allowing Tacitus to reject the theory of Tiberius' physical appearance causing shame, as he had avoided crowds and people earlier in his life during is seclusion on Rhodes.

nudus capillo vertex: 'his head bereft of hair'. A periphrastic presentation of the bald Tiberius. The phraseology, which is virtually poetic, seems to emphasize the ugliness through the juxtaposition of form and content.

ulcerosa facies ac ... medicaminibus interstincta: 'a face full of sores and patched with cosmetics'. **ulcerosa** has the sense of 'blotchy'; *medicamina*, which could also mean 'salves' or 'ointments', is perhaps better treated as 'cosmetics' in order to reflect Tacitus' treatment of Tiberius as one who is wont to dissemble. It is perhaps akin to the Shakespearean phrase 'paint an inch thick'.

et = *et tamen*: 'and yet'. To mark the dismissal of the theory of his physical ugliness influencing his departure from Rome. This use of *et* = *et tamen* is common in Tacitus, e.g. II.86.2.

Rhodi secreto: 'in the seclusion of Rhodes'. Tiberius retreated to Rhodes in 6 BC–AD 2. The reasons for this self-exile are somewhat

A
Level

muddy, but the coincidence of its occurrence with the promotion of Gaius and Lucius, Augustus' grandsons, seems hardly accidental.

57.3

impotentia: 'unruliness'. The relationship between Tiberius and his mother was a complex and confusing one. Her huge influence over her son is unquestionable, though Tacitus is unusually hostile to her, claiming that 'as a mother she was domineering' (*Annals* V.1) and 'more than a match for her son's deviousness' (ibid.). Tiberius also limited honours awarded to her while she was alive (I.14.2). However, the *SCPP* 114–118 and Velleius Paterculus II.130.5 paint a far more positive picture of the relationship between mother and son. For those who would wish to know more about Rome's first 'First lady', see Barrett (2002), *Livia, First Lady of Imperial Rome*; New Haven.

sibi Tiberium adscivit: 'he adopted Tiberius for himself'. This adoption, which took place at the same time as Tiberius' adoption of Germanicus, occurred in AD 4. The conventional understanding is that Augustus sought to guarantee the succession of the Principate for the ensuing generation.

reposcebat: 'she was demanding compensation'. The financial metaphor suggested by the verb perhaps communicates the strained relationship between mother and son.

58.1

Cocceius Nerva: Died in AD 33 and was the grandfather of the emperor Nerva. He was consul with Gaius Vibrius Rufinus in AD 22. He was one of the intimate friends of Tiberius. Nerva accompanied Tiberius in his retirement from Rome in AD 26. In AD 33 he resolutely starved himself to death, despite the entreaties of the emperor. From

A
Level

the accounts of his death (Tacitus, *Annals* VI.26; Dio LVIII.21), we may infer that he was tired of his master.

Curtius Atticus: A Roman *eques* and one of Tiberius' few companions on his retirement to Capri. Six years afterwards, in AD 32, he is mentioned as being a victim of the intrigues of Sejanus, though the account of his removal is in a portion of the *Annals* now missing.

58.2

caelestium: 'astronomy'. Thus **periti caelestium** are 'astrologers'. There are numerous associations of Tiberius with astrology, so Tacitus' inclusion of these 'experts' is cutting.

libens patria careret: 'that he would willingly forego his homeland'. The remark brings to mind Cicero, who favoured *patria carere* in descriptions of his own exile. However, the inclusion of **libens** here marks the contrast between Cicero and Tiberius, with the latter seemingly welcoming the alienation from his people and the business of government.

58.3

mox patuit breve confinium artis et falsi vera quam obscuris tegerentur: 'Soon was revealed the narrow dividing line between skill and falsehood, and in what mysteries the truth was concealed'. Again, note the *variatio* between noun and Indirect Question. The remark presages the coming section on not only the astrologers' remarks, but also the 'accidents' that befall Tiberius.

ceterorum nescii egere: 'they acted in ignorance as regards everything else'. The astrologers do foretell correctly (**haud forte dictum**), but their understanding of why was non-existent. The ensuing Causal Clause makes Tiberius' actions in staying away from Rome seem even more outlandish.

A
Level

adsidens: 'encamping'. The verb has another meaning of 'besieging' which is difficult to overlook here. However, the claims that **saepe moenia urbis adsisens** ('often encamping near the walls of the city') are difficult to corroborate. What is indisputable is that Tiberius never re-entered Rome while he was alive.

59.1

ac forte: 'and by chance'. The phrase returns us to the main narrative from which the content of 58.3 has served as an excursus.

anceps periculum: 'a double-edged danger'. The danger is **anceps** ('double-edged') because it increased the falsities of the rumour (**auxit vana rumoris**) that he may soon die as the astrologers had suggested, but also (**praebuit ipsi materiem**) added strength as to why he should trust Sejanus. Tacitus suggests that the incident at Spelunca allowed for extra safety for Sejanus and extra uncertainty for Tiberius.

amicitiae constantiaeque Seiani magis fideret: 'he should trust more the friendship and reliability of Sejanus'. Given that Tiberius at the outset of his reign had asked for support and assistance (I.11.1), *constantia* would have been a quality in Sejanus that he much cherished. However, Tacitus highlights the irony of the situation below with the remark that Sejanus **quamquam exitiosa suaderet** ('urged destructive things').

Speluncae: Spelunca, the modern Sperlonga, located on the Gulf of Terracina, some 65 miles south of Rome.

mare Amunclanum inter <et> Fundanos montes: 'between the Amyclan Sea and the mountains of Fundi'. Note the **anastrophe** on **inter** to reinforce the seclusion and secrecy of the place.

59.3

adsimulabatque iudicis partis: 'and he assumed the role of a judge ...'. The *–que* suffix serves to link this remark to the observation that

Sejanus was not viewed as **non sui anxius** ('not anxious for himself'), implying that this is his primary purpose in assuring himself of Tiberius' favour. **adsimulabat** further heightens the sense of the theatrical which has dominated Book IV; pretence has now become the norm.

qui accusatorum nomina sustinerent: 'to take up the roles of accusers'. As Sejanus has taken on the role of judge – feigning impartiality – he requires others to assume the role of the accusers against the elder children of Germanicus.

segnitiam iuvenis: 'sluggishness of the young man'. The remark is communicated very much from Sejanus' perspective. The quality of *modestia* is almost antithetical to Sejanus' own nature and shows how much he mocks Nero for his apparent lack of ambition and capability.

60.1

nihil quidem pravae cogitationis: 'there was no trace of a crooked thought'. The 'whiter-than-white' presentation of Nero here, while probably not wholly accurate, nevertheless reinforces the contrasts with Sejanus, and how vulnerable the young man was to his machinations.

voces procebant contumaces et inconsultae: 'utterances would come forth, proud and thoughtless'. The personification of **voces** and the sense of **inconsultae** add to the lack of intent on Nero's part.

diversae insuper sollicitudinum formae oriebantur: 'different and additional scenes of anxiety began to arise'. The theatrical presentation of events continues with **formae**, creating a vivid sense of the events beginning to take on a life of their own, with our stage-manager's scenes in full flight.

A
Level

60.2

vitare ... averti ... abrumpere: 'avoid ... turn away ... break off'. This **tricolon**, mirrored by that of **alius ... quidam ... plerique** ('one man ... some ... most') vividly communicates the growing isolation of Nero.

qui Seiano fautores aderant: 'the men who were present as supporters of Sejanus'. **fautores** again pushes the theatricality as it has the sense not only of political 'supporters', but also theatrical 'fans' or audience members. **Seiano** is Possessive Dative.

enimvero: 'on the other hand ...'. While this could be translated as 'moreover', the adversative sense is perhaps better here to contrast the **torvus aut falsum renidens vultu** ('grim in his expression or smiling falsely') with **insistentibus ... inridentibusque** ('standing by and mocking') attributed to the agents of Sejanus.

cum uxor vigilias ... patefaceret: 'since his wife was disclosing his wakefulness'. The betrayal of his wife Julia, the daughter of Tiberius' son Drusus, whom he had married in AD 20, is the climax of Nero's isolation.

spe obiecta principis loci: 'having thrown before him the hope of the position of princeps'. Sejanus plays brother against brother here, with the presentation of Drusus (III) being far from flattering. The verb *obicio* is seen in various contexts where it is associated with the idea of throwing scraps of food to animals; likewise the noun **insidiis** ('traps') and the adjective **praeferocem** ('high-spirited') are equally applicable to animals. Thus Drusus becomes the faithful hound. It is also telling that he is offered only the **principis loci,** rather than any underlying substance.

si priorem aetate et iam labefactum demovisset: 'if he removed his elder and already weakened sibling'. The phrase seems metaphorical for the destruction of a damaged building, following on from the use of **loci** above.

60.3

cupidinem potentiae et solita fratribus odia accendebatur invidia: 'envy and the customary hatred of brothers enflamed his desire for power'. The phrase calls to mind not only the historic sibling rivalries of Rome, but also the factionalism that plagued the imperial household under Tiberius and the later Julio-Claudians.

ut non in eum quoque semina futuri exitii meditaretur: '... that he did not contemplate the seeds of future destruction against him'. Sejanus is the ultimate puppet-master, whose hand can barely be seen or detected. **semina** is frequently use in the context of destruction.

61: The chapter records the deaths of Asinius Agrippa and Quintus Haterius. The latter serving as an example of an eloquent orator, the lack of whose surviving works is lamented by Tacitus, as has the loss of his style of eloquence, in a pointed comment that 'laborious deliberations' now dominate.

62–63: The account of AD *27 opens with the collapse of an amphitheatre at Fidenae, resulting in the deaths or serious injury of 50,000 people (63.1). Potential* hyperbole *aside, the anecdote serves to illustrate how the Roman people had been 'starved of games' under Tiberius (62.2) and take the first opportunity following his departure to glut their hunger.*

64–65: One disaster is followed hard upon by another: a major fire on the Caelian Hill. Tiberius does deal with the matter in absentia, *by 'distributing money in proportion to the losses' (64.1). The ability to do so speaks volumes about the fiscal responsibility of Tiberius. While his austerity led to a lack of popular support, it cannot be denied that under his administration Rome's coffers were in a very healthy state.*

A
Level

66: A further example of the spate of accusations in the reign of Tiberius,
thus contributing to Tacitus' presentation of a tyrannical state. He notes
that Quintilius Varus' fate was not decided at this time, with the Senate
'voting to wait for the Emperor, the one temporary refuge from the
pressing evils' (66.2). Thus Tiberius' absence is presented here in
providing a stay of execution for Varus, but also highlights how his
absence impairs the normal course of senatorial action.

67 (AD 27)

This chapter covers Tiberius' withdrawal to Capri. Tacitus' presentation
of Capri features a number of specific geographical descriptions,
suggesting that Capri is unfamiliar to his readership. This is certainly
not the case, given that the Bays of Naples and Baiae served as a
playground for Rome's elite. The specificity of his description is
deliberate, as it reinforces the distance that Tiberius has withdrawn
from Rome – metaphorically, if not literally. Dio (LVIII.5.1) remarks
that, at this point in time, Sejanus seemed to be more like the emperor,
while Tiberius was regarded as 'some form of off-shore monarch'.
Suetonius (*Tib.* 41–44) provides a reasonably full catalogue of the
sexual and immoral acts that Tiberius allegedly enjoyed in his
seclusion. Dio (LVIII.22.1) also alludes to 'the sensual orgies which
he carried on shamelessly'. Velleius Paterculus (II.126.1–128.4) is far
more positive on the period, and indeed on the relationship between
Tiberius and Sejanus, although his contemporary nature and his
owing of his own political career to the Principate both limit his
reliability.

67.1

at Caesar: 'But Caesar'. Following the events of chapters 62–66,
primarily the collapse of an amphitheatre at Fidenae and a large fire

on the Caelian Hill at Rome, Tacitus returns his focus to the emperor himself. The forceful conjunction **at** emphasizes that the emperor is elsewhere, with the implication that he is not fulfilling his role. Suetonius (*Tib.* 41.1) likewise tells us that Tiberius 'let all affairs of state slide'.

dedicatis per Campaniam templis: 'having dedicated the temples throughout Campania'. See chapter 57 on the fact that these were dedicated 'under the pretence (*specie*)' of religion.

quamquam edicto monuisset: 'although he had warned by edict'. *edictum* will become a key word in the subsequent accounts of Tiberius' reign in both Tacitus and Dio. In residence on Capri, letters and bulls became the prime means of the emperor expressing his wishes.

perosus tamen: 'however, disgusted with ...'. **perosus** is a powerful word to express Tiberius' sentiments. While it could be translated as 'weary with', as a compound of *odi*, a stronger sense of dislike is needed in the English. **tamen** here seems to co-ordinate with **quamquam** above: the implication is that although demanding peace and quiet, this was not as forthcoming as was wished; thus *tamen* marks the spontaneous escalation of his odium.

municipia et colonias omniaque in continenti sita: 'the municipalities and colonies and everything else situated on the mainland'. The polysyndetic tricolon here (**municipia ... colonias ... omnia**) should be obvious to all readers. municipia et coloniae is common phrasing to refer to all the towns of Italy collectively. The more generic **omnia** adds a touch of hyperbole.

Capreas se in insulam abdidit: 'he hid himself away on the island of Capri'. The syntax here mirrors the sense. **Capreas** would typically follow **in insulam**: its promotion in the clause not only juxtaposes it with the preceding tricolon, but allows for the sandwiching of the reflexive pronoun.

trium milium freto ab extremis Surrentini promunturii diiunctam: 'cut off from the Surrentine promontory by a strait of three miles'. The degree of akribeia here is striking, reinforcing the conscious choice of location by Tiberius.

solitudinem eius placuisse maxime crediderim: 'I would believe that the isolation that pleased him the most'. See 41.3 on the fact that Sejanus exploited this very desire for solitude. **crediderim** is perfect subjunctive for potential.

importuosum circa mare: 'the surrounding sea is harbourless'. **circa** here is adjectival, so one could not really speak of anastrophe. The description is designed, along with **vix modicis navigiis pauca subsida** ('scarcely landing points even for little boats') below, to conjure an imposing and hostile approach. Suetonius (*Tib.* 40) describes Capri in very similar terms: 'having only one small landing beach – the remainder of its coast consisting of sheer cliffs surrounded by deep water'. The inference one is forced to draw is that Tiberius has selected a refuge that has a 'personality' similar to his own.

aestas in favonium obversa: 'its summer [aspect] faces the west winds'. **aestas** here is striking as an example of metonymy, meaning in reality 'the island in summer'.

aperto circum pelago peramoena: 'with the open sea around, it is very beautiful'. Here there is a notable anastrophe on **circum**. **peramoena** conjures the idea of an idyllic location, with the intensifying prefix (*per-*) being unique here with *amoenus*.

antequam Vesuvius mons ardescens faciem loci verteret: 'before the erupting Mount Vesuvius changed the appearance of the place'. The clause alludes to the major eruption of AD 79.

A
Level

fama tradit: 'Report passes it down . . .'. This formula is typical among historians and other authors when dealing with pseudo-mythological proto-history. It absolves the author of error, whilst elevating the tone of the Latin to a quasi-poetical quality.

sed tum Tiberius duodecim villarum † nominibus et molibus † insederat: 'but now Tiberius settled there in twelve † huge individually-named † villas'.

occultior in luxus et malum otium resolutus: 'his more concealed relaxation into luxuriousness and wicked idleness.' **occultior** is very much in keeping with the presentation of Tiberius as secretive. **luxus et malum otium** allows for Tacitus to take the moral high ground, as both of these were seen as anathema to 'traditional' Roman attitudes. Interestingly, Suetonius (*Tib.* 34) claims that Tiberius took stringent action against luxuriousness in his edicts and public façade, thus here we may also see the charge of hypocrisy, given that Tacitus' comments on his **intentus olim publicas ad curas** ('previous attentiveness to public matters'); note the two clauses being coordinated by **quanto . . . tanto**.

manebat quippe suspicionem et credendi temeritas: 'To be sure there yet remained his rashness in suspicion and gullibility . . .'. Note the *variatio* of accusative noun ~ genitive gerund. Sejanus will exploit further these two complementary aspects of Tiberius' nature.

non iam occultis ... insidiis: 'traps no longer concealed'. The immediate ascendancy of Sejanus now being secured, his boldness increases beyond the need for obfuscation.

miles: 'soldiery'. Collective singular.

nuntios, introitus aperta, secreta: 'their messages, visits, disclosures, secrets'. The asyndetic list provides a telling snapshot of the web of informers operated by Sejanus in his persecution of Agrippina, Nero, and Drusus (III).

A
Level

velut in annales referebat: 'as if in their annals'. The precise meaning of **annales** is unclear here. It cannot simply refer to 'log-books', as **velut** neutralizes this interpretation. It may be an allusion to the minutiae of information to which Sejanus had access.

ultroque struebantur qui monerent perfugere ad Germaniae exercitus: 'and in addition people were set up to advise them to flee to the armies in Germany'. A further plot of Sejanus, where he has agents deliberately giving incriminating advice to Agrippina and her sons. Had they acted on this advice, the interpretation would necessarily have been treasonous; a similar situation would have been the interpretation placed upon **celeberrimo fori effigiem divi Augusti amplecti** ('to embrace the statue of the Divine Augustus in the throng of the forum'). **ultro** here is the sense of 'on top of everything else'; **qui** is to be read as replacing the *ut* in a Purpose Clause.

68–71 (AD 28)

As we move towards the denouement of Book IV, Tacitus does not allow either the suspense or the vividness of his narration to abate. These chapters are concerned with the friends of Germanicus in Rome, and their suffering at the hands of Sejanus and his cronies. The key figure is Titius Sabinus, whose entrapment is one of the most affecting passages in the *Annals*. His naivety and eventual downfall contribute to a general anxiety in Rome which culminates in the near-total breakdown of the social norms of the city.

68.1

Iunio Silano et Silio Nerva consulibus: 'With Junius Silanus and Silius Nerva as consuls …'. C. Appius Junius Silanus was himself accused of maiestas in AD 32; his eventual murder in AD 42 at the hands of the Claudian freedman Narcissus, is mentioned briefly at XI.29.1. Of Silius Nerva, nothing else is known.

foedum anni principium incessit: 'a foul beginning to the year came about'. The clause itself is rather vague, as **foedum** could apply to numerous contexts, including that of weather. It is only with the reveal in the ensuing Ablative Absolute that we understand the context of persecution and moral outrage that Tacitus wishes to conjure.

inlustri equite Romano: 'the illustrious Roman equestrian'. The contrast with the tone of the description of Sejanus' background at IV.1.2 is rather pointed.

ob amicitiam Germanici: 'on account of his friendship with Germanicus'. Sabinus' case had been deferred from AD 24 (IV.19.1), at the time when Sosia Galla had been arrested also. *amicitia* is a key concept for these chapters.

neque . . . omiserat . . . percolere: 'he had not omitted to be courteous'. **Litotes** to stress the iniquity of the charge against Sabinus.

post tot clientes unus: 'the only one [left] after so many clients'. The **juxtaposition** heightens the obvious contrast.

eoque apud bonos laudatus et gravis iniquis: 'and hence praised among good men and disagreeable to the unjust'. The chiasmus here, combined with the *variatio* of **apud** + acc. ~ dat. stresses the antithetical qualities of Sabinus to Sejanus.

68.2

Latinius Latiaris, Porcius Cato, Petilius Rufus, M. Opsius: This list of names in the nominative is evocative of the scale of persecution directed at Sabinus. The effect of conspiracy that it creates is unmistakeable. Little is known of these individuals save for Porcius

Cato, who was suffect consul in AD 36 and curator aquarum in AD 38. In that year he also seems to have been executed by the emperor Gaius. Tacitus (see below IV.71.1) alludes to his accounts of the deaths of these prosecutors, so it seems that they were recorded in the books of the *Annals* now lost.

cupidine consulatus: 'in their desire for the consulship'. The alliteration to emphasize that this is done out of the hope for personal gain, rather than any sense of moral duty of desire for justice.

ad quem non nisi per Seianum aditus: 'to which there was no access save through Sejanus'. Dio (LVIII.4.1) also attests to the pre-eminence of Sejanus. By controlling access to Tiberius, Sejanus was now the de facto power in Rome. Dio adds that he had 'gained the favour of the senators, partly by the benefits he conferred, partly by the hopes he inspired, and partly by intimidation' (LVIII.4.2).

neque Seiani voluntas nisi scelere quaerebatur: 'nor was the blessing of Sejanus to be acquired save through crime'. Note the repeated pattern of **non nisi per Seianum ... neque Seiani ... nisi**, which stresses the centrality of the man to all things in Rome. *scelum* reinforces the corruption that Sejanus has created in Rome, as others seek to be as opportunistic in their acquisition of influence as he has been. The moral degradation that comes with this is in stark contrast to the traditional view of Roman qualities (see, for example, Sallust *in Catalinam* 9.2: *cives cum civibus de virtute certabant* – 'citizens contested with citizens over virtue').

Latiaris ... strueret dolum: 'Latiaris should set out the snare'. The choice of **dolum** is deliberate, conjuring ideas not only of hunters and prey, but also trickery, flummery and deceit. The ensuing stages of the plot, and its gradual progress, reveal just how involved the downfall of Sabinus was.

68.3

ut sunt molles in calamitate mortalium animi: 'as the spirits of mortals are soft in misfortune'. The generalizing observation by Tacitus serves to place the sympathies of the reader with Sabinus, by making his actions seem universally intelligible.

saevitiam, superbiam, spes eius: 'his savagery, arrogance, and ambitions'. The sibilance is unquestionably deliberate. It fulfils a double purpose, evoking not only the whispering of Sabinus – who believes that he has found a confidante – but also the venom of his feeling against Sejanus.

68.4

tamquam vetita miscuissent: 'as if they had exchanged treasonable utterances'. This is patently not the case, as any remarks of Latiaris would be simply entrapment.

speciem artae amicitiae fecere: 'effected the appearance of close friendship'. The re-occurrence of *species* is of course significant, especially here in association with *amicitia*. The implication Tacitus makes is that even the most entrenched socio-political customs are perverted by Sejanus. **fecere** is the syncopated Third Person Plural perfect.

quasi ad fidissimum: 'as if to the most faithful of men'. **quasi** necessarily maintains the idea of illusion.

69.1

nam loco, in quem coibatur, servanda solitudinis facies: 'For the place in which they would meet had to keep the appearance of solitude'. **coibatur** = *coituri erant* (see *NLS* §200 (ii)). **facies** again evokes the theatrical styling of the Sejanus episodes, with this moment in particular appearing as a set-piece.

A
Level

haud minus turpi latebra quam detestanda fraude: 'in a lair no less disgusting than their treachery was hateful'. The phraseology of this section is very vivid and equally damning. The three senators creep about like vermin between roof and ceiling (**tectum inter et laquearia**); their location is one as filled with squalor as their morals are lacking; and they all seem to press their ears to every available crack (**foraminibus et rimis aurem admovent**).

69.2

velut recens cognita narraturus: 'as if about to tell some fresh information'. **velut** continues the imagery of falsity. The future participle expressing purpose here.

quorum adfatim copia: 'of which there was an abundant supply'. Referring to the 'past and present instances' (**praeteritaque et instantia**) of Sejanus' offences. A telling authorial comment.

69.3

non alias magis anxia et pavens civitas: 'At no other time was the citizen-body more tense and panicked'. Perhaps a touch of hyperbole, but Tacitus' point is well-made.

<cautissime> agens adversum proximos: 'acting most cautiously towards those closest to them'.

etiam muta atque inanima, tectum et parietes circumspectabantur: 'even mute and inanimate objects, [such as] a roof and walls, were considered with suspicion.' This phrase adequately sums up the climate of fear that now dominates Roman society. The phrase 'the walls have ears' would be a modern equivalent.

70.1

sollemnia incipientis anni kalendis Ianuariis: 'solemn prayers for the beginning year on the Kalends of January'. i.e. 1 January. The assignment of the year's beginning to the month of January is probably datable to the decemvirate of 451–450 BC, but Roman tradition assigned it to the calendrical reforms of Numa Pompilius, Rome's second king. The day was considered the ultimate *dies fastus*, thus Tiberius' usurpation of the business of the day for his accusation of Sabinus seems something of a sacrilege in Tacitus' eyes.

epistula: 'by letter'. See above on 67.1 on the isolation Tiberius enjoyed on Capri.

corruptos quosdam libertorum et petitum se arguens: 'charging him that certain of his freedmen had been corrupted and that he himself [i.e. Tiberius] was the target'. These accusations differ greatly from the **ob amicitiam Germanici** above. Perhaps the charges are invented, or perhaps the actual historicity of the event did not suit Tacitus' dramatic purposes as well.

ultionemque haud obscure poscebat: 'he was demanding vengeance with no lack of clarity'. The virtual double negative of **haud obscure** stands in stark contrast to Tiberius' typical obfuscation.

clamitans sic inchoari annum, has Seiano victimas cadere: 'shouting that thus was the year being begun, that these were the victims felled for Sejanus'. **cadere** is the technical term for the killing of sacrificial victims. Part of the festal programme for the inauguration of the new year involved the sacrificing of bulls to Jupiter. Sabinus' exclamation twists this to emphasize that Sejanus is now the real 'power'.

70.2

intendisset ... acciderent: 'he directed ... they fell'. The subjunctives are frequentative, i.e. they generalize the observations. Thus the two instances of **quo** (note the anaphora) need to be translated as 'wherever'.

A
Level

deseri itinera, fora: 'the streets, the fora, were deserted'. The day-to-day of Rome has been utterly brought down by Sejanus' actions. A similar observation was made at II.82.3, where at the news of Germanicus' death 'the fora were deserted, houses shut', but while the latter was a show of respect, the current situation is conditioned by fear.

id ipsum paventes quod timuissent: 'fearing the very fact that they had been afraid'. **Synonymia**. The people only re-appear when they realize that, by being perceived as being afraid, they too may be in danger of prosecution.

70.3

quem enim diem: 'For what day . . .'. oratio obliqua (without formal introductory verb).

71.1

ni mihi destinatum foret suum quaeque in annum referre: 'If it were not my design to record events each in their own year . . .'. This remark is quite common in Tacitus who, by following an annalistic history, has limited control over his chronology. However, here he enjoys the best of both worlds: by hinting that the outcomes (**exitus**) of the various accusers of Sabinus are particularly exciting, thus adding a frisson of expectation for his later account. Latiaris was killed in AD 32, and Tacitus mentions his record of the death at VI.4.1. We must surmise then that the Tacitean accounts of these 'outcomes' were contained in the missing books covering Gaius' reign.

satiatus et oblatis in eandem operam recentibus: 'when he [Tiberius] was glutted and new men were available for the same task'. The imagery here is quite striking and suggests the uninterrupted process of persecution that Tiberius (in Tacitus' opinion) operated. **satiatus** evokes the bloodthirstiness of the emperor; this could, when read alongside other vocabulary in this section, **repertores** ('devisers') and **ministros** ('deliverers'), conjure an image of 'execution to order'. The constant replacement of the **ministros** (**oblatis recentibus**) is also suggestive of Tiberius' need for not only effective assistants, but also the thrill of new modes of entrapment and accusation.

veteres et praegraves adflixit: '... he cast them down as old and clumsy'. The limited lifespan of these **repertores** is highlighted here. The two adjectives are evocative of animals past their prime; the idea of these individuals being 'put out of their misery' is unmistakeable.

71.2

Asinius Gallus: Gaius Asinius Gallus Saloninus is perhaps the most frequently mentioned senator in the Tiberian books, seemingly because he serves as the sole remaining 'independent' voice at times. Having been consul in 8 BC, both his career and personal life brought him into conflict with Tiberius. Tacitus (*Annals* I.12.2) gives Gallus some particularly sarcastic remarks at Tiberius accession, which doubtless marked Gallus as a troublemaker. However, the more personal enmity perhaps developed from the fact that in 11 BC Gallus married Vipsania, Tiberius' first wife, whom he had been forced to divorce in order to marry Julia, the daughter of Augustus. If this were not enough, following Vipsania's death (AD 20), Gallus also seems to have courted Agrippina, Germanicus' widow. This catalogue of associations would have certainly attracted the attention of Tiberius. In AD 30, Tiberius had the Senate declare him a public enemy, whereupon he was imprisoned, eventually dying of starvation in AD 33. Dio (LVIII.3.1–3.6) also gives an account of Gallus' arrest.

cuius liberorum Agrippina matertera erat: 'of whose children Agrippina was the maternal aunt'. Vipsania and Agrippina were half-sisters, both being daughters of Agrippa.

A
Level

71.3

nullam aeque ... quam dissimulationem diligebat: 'he cherished nothing as much as his dissimulation'. The fact that Tiberius sees this as one of his virtues (**ut rebatur**) is entirely in keeping with Tacitus' presentation of the princeps.

tristibus dictis atrocia facta coniungere: '... he joined savage actions to his bitter words'. The idiom *dictum ~ factum* is proverbial for speed. While Tiberius is typically plodding (**cunctationes**), when in a fit of anger (**prorupisset**) his rage is accompanied by not only words, but also actions of a horrific nature.

71.4

Iulia mortem obiit: 'Julia met her death'. This is Julia the Younger (*c*.19 BC – AD 28), daughter of Julia and Agrippa and thus granddaughter of Augustus. She had been exiled in AD 8 (see *Annals* III.24) for adultery, which flew in the face of Augustus' moral legislation.

quae florentes privignos cum per occultum subvertisset: 'who had secretly undermined her stepchildren as they flourished'. This is the allegation that Livia (Augusta), the wife of Augustus, had engaged in a campaign of enmity against the other potential successors in order that her own child, Tiberius, might succeed. Tacitus alleges that she had a hand in the deaths of Gaius and Lucius Caesar (*Annals* I.3.3) and Agrippa Postumus (*Annals* I.6.2); Suetonius (*Tib.* 22) also inculcates her in the death of Agrippa Postumus. Dio (LVI.30.2) even suggests that she may have been responsible for the death of Augustus himself. Whatever the truth of this, Livia was certainly a powerful and fascinating woman.

72–73: Tacitus' account of the Frisian revolt opens with his observation that it was prompted 'more because of our greed than [their] intolerance of compliance' (72.1). The revolt therefore serves to illustrate a moral point, where a formerly peaceful tribe are pushed into rebellion by Roman outrages and mismanagement. The fact that the Frisians also manage to defeat the Romans also highlights the weakness of Rome at this stage, which Tacitus would have us believe is due to the moral corruption of Tiberius and Sejanus.

74 (AD 28)

The penultimate chapter of Book IV brings us back almost full circle to the character and ambitions of Sejanus that dominated the opening chapters. The focus is placed on the construction of altars honouring the relationship between Tiberius and Sejanus, followed by an account of the people flocking to Campania to try to catch a glimpse of Sejanus. The elevation of Sejanus to quasi-divine status is a necessary precursor to his fall; his hubris must reach its climax. But perhaps more than an attack on Sejanus himself, here Tacitus directs his ferocity to the sycophancy of the people of Rome, in particular the Senate, who have not merely allowed the rise of Sejanus, but actively pandered to him out of a mix of selfishness and fear. We should remember the remark attributed to Tiberius at *Annals* III.65, describing the senators as 'men primed for slavery'. Their willing acquiescence to Sejanus is perhaps indicative of the accuracy of this statement. For another account of the pinnacle of Sejanus' power, see Dio LVIII.4.1–5.7.

74.1

clarum inde . . . Frisum nomen: 'The name of the Frisians was famous thereafter . . .'. The Frisii lived in the area bordered by the Ijssel Meer, i.e. the low-lying region between the Rhine–Meuse–Scheldt delta and the River Ems. Tiberius' brother Drusus had first made agreements with the Frisii, but subsequently they had been overtaxed and abused by the Romans. This culminated in AD 28, when the tribe rebelled

A
Level

against Rome, even defeating a Roman army (under the command of Lucius Apronius) at the Battle of Baduhenna Wood. Tacitus gave an account of these events in chapters 72–73.

dissimulante Tiberio damna: 'with Tiberius covering up the damage'. Once again Tiberius engages in deception, here – as Tacitus would have us believe – so that no one could gain glory by successfully campaigning against them.

neque senatus in eo cura, an imperii extrema dehonestarentur: 'nor was it a concern of the Senate that the edges of the empire were being dishonoured'. Again Tacitus makes his observation that the traditional ways of Roman behaviour are being ignored or abused. We need only think of Virgil *Aeneid* VI.851–3 or Sallust *in Catalinam* 7.4–7 for the ways in which Romans 'should' behave towards aggressors.

pavor internus occupaverat animos: 'domestic panic had occupied their minds'. The pluperfect here suggests the length of time that this has afflicted the politicians of Rome. When we contrast this with the apparent lack of concern over the Frisii, we are forced to confront the psychological terror which Sejanus and Tiberius have imposed upon Rome.

cui remedium adulatione quaerebatur: 'for which a remedy was trying to be sought through sycophancy'. **quaerebatur** is to be treated as Conative, as even the sycophancy of the Senate does not bring them any real solace. The phrase is to be contrasted with **remedium ex bello** (72.3), which was the solution sought by the Frisii. There is an irony marked here by Tacitus that it is the barbarian 'other' who has taken the more 'Roman' solution.

74.2

aram clementiae, aram amicitiae: 'an Altar of Clemency, an Altar of Friendship'. Clemency (*clementia*) was a key concept for the emperor. Augustus (then Octavian) had famously demonstrated his clemency after the Battle of Actium, where he had 'forgiven' the Roman soldiers who had fought with Marc Antony (Velleius Paterculus II.86); Seneca wrote a treatise, the *De clementia*, as an instructional text for the young Nero; Dio (LIX.16.10) tells us that the Senate passed a resolution offering annual sacrifices to the clemency of Gaius, simply because he had not put them to death. This last example is perhaps the same in tone to our current section of Tacitus.

The Altar of Friendship is a physical symbol of the close relationship between Sejanus and Tiberius, whose *amicitia* has dominated Book IV. Note the anaphora of aram.

74.3

satis visum omittere insulam: 'it seemed sufficient merely to quit the island'. Even amid public clamour and adoration, Tiberius refuses to return to Rome, but does deign to visit Campania at least (*in proximo Campaniae*).

eo venire patres, eques, magna pars plebis: 'Hither came the senators, the equestrians, a great part of the plebs'. The asyndetic list, including the collective singular eques, starkly marks the sycophancy of the people. The fact that they make a pilgrimage to Campania simply to catch a glimpse of Sejanus and Tiberius serves to elevate them even further in status. In Sejanus' case this is wholly abhorrent to Tacitus. Note above the mention of **crebris precibus** ('frequent prayers'): while this could be translated as 'entreaties', the use of 'prayers' seems to fit rather better with the quasi-religious overtones of the Latin.

74.4

foedum illud in propatulo servitium: 'that servile filth in his courtyard'. **in propatulo** could be translated simply as 'in the open', corresponding to the sense of 'in plain sight', but this translation makes the association of the adorants more personal to Sejanus. Dio

(LVIII.5.2) notes the frequent 'anxious jostling around Sejanus' doors', while at LVIII.5.5 a couch collapses under the weight of the number of people waiting to see him. The judgement here is not that of Tacitus, but rather is written from the perspective of Sejanus himself, in keeping with his increasing arrogance (**auctam ei adrogantiam**).

campo aut litore ... noctem ac diem ... gratiam aut fastus ianitorum: 'on the plain or on the shore . . . night or day . . . the favour or disdain of his doorkeepers'. The tricolon of alternatives here reinforces the eagerness of the sycophants. Doorkeepers (*ianitores*) were traditionally arrogant in Latin literature, featuring heavily in the paraklausithyron ('lament of the locked-out lover') sub-genre of love elegy (see, for example, Ovid *Amores* I.6); but here the scale of their haughtiness is correlative with that of their master Sejanus.

74.5

infaustae amicitiae: 'unpropitious friendship'. A pithy summation of the situation, not only relevant to the quasi-religious nature of the chapter, but also to the theme of *amicitia* in the whole Book. *infaustus* is often seen in association with omens, e.g. *auspicium*, Virgil, *Aeneid* XI.347. Here the friendship is 'unpropitious' as, after Sejanus' fall, the reprisals against his associates will be vicious. Dio (LVIII.10.4) points out how quickly some sought to distance themselves from 'the man whose friendship they had formerly cherished'.

75 (the end of AD 28)

The year ends with a very brief mention of the marriage between Agrippina the Younger, daughter of Germanicus, and Gn. Domitius Ahenobarbus. The fact that Tiberius personally blesses this union may seem innocuous, and Tacitus seemingly gives little real attention to it, but it is a particularly significant moment. Given that in the course of Book IV Sejanus has been forbidden to marry Livilla, the public celebration of this imperial marriage must have given him pause for thought. Moreover, the reader will – by virtue of the names alone – pick up on the fact that Tacitus once again foreshadows his later writing: Books XII.64 to the end of the surviving text of the *Annals*. For the son born of this union will be none other than the Emperor Nero.

75

cum coram . . . tradidisset: 'when he had personally handed over . . .'. It would not be too far of a stretch to suggest that, by using **coram**, Tacitus is in part blaming Tiberius for Nero. Suetonius (*Nero* 6.1) informs us that Nero was born nine months after Tiberius' death; his father is alleged to have remarked that 'any child born to himself and Agrippina was bound to have a detestable nature and become a public danger'.

Vocabulary

An asterisk * denotes a word in OCR's Defined Vocabulary List for AS.

*a, ab (+ abl.)	from, by
abdo, abdere, abdidi, abditus	remove, set aside
abnuo, abnuere, abnui, abnuitus	refuse, deny guilt
abrumpo, abrumpere, abrupi, abruptus	break off
abscessus, abscessus, m.	withdrawal, departure
abstineo, abstinere, abstinui, abstentus	abstain
abstrudo, abstrudere, abstrusi, abstrusus	thrust away
*absum, abesse, afui	be absent, be away, be distant
*ac, atque (indeclinable)	and
accendo, accendere, accendi, accensus	set on fire, enflame
*accido, accidere, accidi	happen
*accipio, accipere, accepi, acceptus	accept, take in, receive, hear
accusatio, accusationis, f.	indictment, charge
accusator, accusatoris, m.	accuser, prosecutor
accuso, accusare, accusavi, accusatus	accuse, charge
*acer, acris, acre	keen, sharp, fierce
*ad (+ acc.)	to, towards, at, about, near
adcelero, adcelerare, adceleravi, adceleratus	speed up, accelerate
adcursus, adcursus, m.	a rushing up to
*addo, addere, addidi, additus	add, join
*adeo (indeclinable)	so much, so greatly, to such an extent
adfatim (indeclinable)	sufficiently
adflictus, adflicta, adflictum	shattered, afflicted
adfligo, adfligere, adflixi, adflictus	strike, throw down
adfluens, adfluens	overflowing
*adhuc (indeclinable)	till now, still
*adimo, adimere, ademi, ademptus	take away, remove

*adipiscor, adipisci, adeptus sum	obtain
aditus, aditus, m.	approach, right to approach
adiungo, adiungere, adiunxi, adjuntus	add, join to
adiutor, adiutoris, m.	assistant, accomplice
adloquium, adloquii, n.	address, talk
admoneo, admonere, admonui, admonitus (+ gen.)	remind, draw attention to
adpello, adpellere, adpuli, adpulsus	put ashore at
adpositus, adposita, adpositum	near, adjacent, placed near
adprendo, adprendere, adprendi, adprensus	seize upon, take hold of
adrogantia, adrogantiae, f.	arrogance
adscisco, adsciscere, adscivi, adscitus	adopt, appropriate
adseveratio, adseverationis, f.	affirmation
adsideo, adsidere, adsedi, adsessus	watch over
adsiduus, adsidua, adsiduum	unremitting, regularly in attendance
adsimulo, adsimulare, adsimulavi, adsimulatus	simulate, pretend, counterfeit
adsisto, adsistere, adstiti, adstatus	stand nearby
*adsum, adesse, adfui	be here, be present
adulatio, adulationis, f.	fawning, flattery, adulation
*adulescens, adulescentis, m.	youth, young man
adulterium, adulteri, m.	adulterer
adulterium, adulterii, n.	adultery
adultus, adulta, adultum	adult
adversor, adversari, adversatus sum	act contrary to, oppose
*adversus (+ acc.)	against, towards
aemulatio, aemulationis, f.	rivalry, imitation, emulation
aemulus, aemuli, m	rival, competitor
aeque (indeclinable)	in an equal degree
*aequus, aequa, aequum	equal, fair, favourable, calm
aestas, aestatis, f.	summer
aestimo, aestimare, aestimavi, aestimatus	value, reckon, consider, hold
aetas, aetatis, f.	lifetime, age
*aggredior, aggredi, aggressus sum (also adgredior)	attack, approach
*ago, agere, egi, actus	do, act, drive

gratias ago	thank, give thanks
aio (lacking in most forms)	say
alacer, alacris, alacre	joyous, lively
alioqui (indeclinable)	otherwise, besides
***aliquis, aliquid**	someone, something, anyone, anything
***alius, alia, aliud**	other, one, another, else
alii . . . alii	some . . . others
altar, altaris, n.	altar
***altus, alta, altum**	high, deep
ambitus, ambitus, m.	a canvassing
amicitia, amicitiae, f.	friendship
***amicus, amici m.**	friend
***amitto, amittere, amisi, amissus**	lose
***amo, amare, amavi, amatus**	love, like
amoenus, amoena, amoenum	beautiful, pleasant
amplector, amplecti, amplexus sum	surround, embrace
***an (indeclinable)**	or
anceps, anceps (gen. ancipitis)	lit. 'two-headed'; double-edged, uncertain, unclear
***angustus, angusta, angustum**	narrow, confined
***animus, animi, m.**	spirit, soul, mind, courage
annalis, annalis, m.	historical work, history
anus, anus, f.	old woman
***annus, anni, m.**	year
***ante (+ acc.)**	before, in front of
***antea (indeclinable)**	before, previously
antehabeo, antehabere, antehabui, antehabitus (+ dat.)	prefer
anteo, antire, anti(v)i, antitus	precede, go farther in front
***antequam (indeclinable)**	before
anxius, anxia, axium	anxious
***aperio, aperire, aperui, apertus**	open, reveal, disclose
apiscor, apisci, aptus sum	obtain, gain
appello, appellare, appellavi, appellatus	speak to, appeal to, support
appono, apponere, apposui, appositus	place nearby

*apud (+ acc.)	among, at the house of, according to, in the opinion of
*ara, arae, f.	altar
arbiter, arbitri, m.	judge, observer
arceo, arcere, arcui	ward off, keep off
ardeo, ardere, arsi, arsus	burn
ardesco, ardescere, arsi	catch fire, ignite
arduus, ardua, arduum	hard, difficult
arguo, arguere, argui, argutus	allege, assert, criticise
*ars, artis, f.	art, skill
artus, arta, artum	close, narrow
aspernor, aspernari, aspernatus sum	despise
aspicio, aspicere, aspexi, aspectus	look at, observe
*at (indeclinable)	but
atrox, atrox	alarming, frightful, terrible
attingo, attingere, attigi, attactus	touch, reach
attollo, attollere	raise up, exalt
auctor, auctoris, m.	author, authority, historian
audacia, audaciae, f.	boldness
*audax, audacis	bold, daring
*audeo, audere, ausus sum	dare
audenter (indeclinable)	boldly
*audio, audire, audivi, auditus	hear, listen to
*aufero, auferre, abstuli, ablatus	take away, carry off, steal
*augeo, augere, auxi, auctus	increase, exaggerate
auris, auris, f.	ear
*aut (indeclinable)	or, either
*autem (indeclinable)	but, however
*auxilium, auxilii, n.	help; (pl.) (auxiliary) troops
aveo, avere	desire eagerly, long for
averto, avertere, averti, aversus	(passive with a reflexive sense) turn away from
avia, aviae, f.	grandmother
avide (indeclinable)	greedily, eagerly
avunculus, avunculi, m.	uncle
*bellum, belli, n.	war
beneficium, beneficii, n.	kindness, service, favour
benevolentia, benevolentiae, f.	kindness, benevolence
*bonus, bona, bonum	good

*brevis, breve	short, brief
*cado, cadere, cecidi, casus	fall, perish
*caedes, caedis, f.	slaughter, killing, murder
caelestis, caeleste	heavenly
caelestis, caelestis, m.	deity, god
*caelum, caeli, n.	sky, heaven
calamitas, calamitatis, f.	misfortune, calamity
callidus, callida, callidum	shrewd, clever, crafty, sly, cunning
*campus, campi, m.	plain, field
capesso, capessere, capessivi, capessitus	grasp, undertake
capillus, capilli, m.	hair
*capio, capere, cepi, captus (in compounds -icio)	take, catch, capture
carcer, carceris, n.	prison
careo, carere, carui, caritus (usually with ablative)	be without, deny oneself (something)
caritas, caritatis, f.	charity, love, affection
*carus, cara, carum	dear
*castra, castrorum, n. pl.	camp
casus, casus, m.	accident, misfortune
*causa, causae, f.	cause, reason, case
causa (+ gen.)	for the sake of
cautus, cauta, cautum	cautious, circumspect, wary
*caveo, cavere, cavi, cautus	beware (of), take care
*cedo, cedere, cessi, cessus	yield, give up; (in compounds) go
celeber, celebris, celebre	frequented, crowded
celebro, celebrare, celebravi, celbratus	celebrate
censeo, censere, censui, census	decree, propose
*centurio, centurionis, m.	centurion
*cerno, cernere, crevi, cretus	see, perceive, decree
*certamen, certaminis, n.	contest, battle, struggle
*certus, certa, certum	certain, sure, fixed
*ceteri, ceterae, cetera	the rest, the other
*cibus, cibi, m.	food
*circum, circa (+ acc.)	around, about
circumspecto, circumspectare, circumspectavi, circumspectatus	look around at, observe carefully

*civitas, civitatis, f.	citizenship, state, city, tribe
clamito, clamitare, clamitavi, clamitatus	cry out
*clamo, clamare, clamavi, clamatus	shout, exclaim, proclaim
*clamor, clamoris, m.	shout, uproar, noise
claresco, clarescere, clarui	become clear, become famous
*clarus, clara, clarum	clear, famous, distinguished
clementia, clementiae, f.	clemency
cliens, clientis, m.	client
codicillus, codicilli, m.	writing tablet, letter
coeo, coire, coi(v)i, coitus	come together, conspire
*coepi, coepisse, coeptus	began
coetus, coetus, m	assemblage, crowd, circle of people
cogitatio, cogitationis, f.	thinking, reflection
*cognosco, cognoscere, cognovi, cognitus	get to know, find out, learn
*cohors, cohortis, f.	cohort, company
collega, collegae, m.	colleague
*colo, colere, colui, cultus	cultivate, worship, honour
colonia, coloniae, f.	colony, a settlement founded by Rome
*comes, comitis, m. and f.	comrade, companion
comis, come	courteous, obliging
comitatus, comitatus, m.	company of soldiers, retinue, entourage
commentarium, commentarii, n.	private journal, commentary
commeo, commeare, commeavi, commeatus	visit, come and go
commotus, commota, commotum	excited, nervous
communis, commune	common, joint, shared
compello, compellare, compellavi, compellatus	address
comperio, comperire, comperi, compertus	find out, know well, find (to have committed an offence)
compleo, complere, complevi, completus	fill up
complexus, complexus, m.	a surrounding, embrace
compono, componere, composui, compositus	arrange, settle

concedo, concedere, concessi, concessus	depart, retire, withdraw
concordia, concordiae, f.	harmony
concursus, concursus, m.	running to and fro
conditor, conditoris, m.	founder
conduco, conducere, conduxi, conductus	be of use, bring together
*confero, conferre, contuli, conlatus	collect, compare, contribute, bestow
confinium, confinii, n.	border, boundary, connection
confirmo, confirmare, confirmavi, confirmatus	establish, strengthen
congressus, congressus, m.	meeting
coniecto, coniectare, coniectavi, coniectatus	conjecture, speculate
coniunctio, coniunctionis, f.	union, fellowship, a joining
*coniunx, coniugis, m. and f.	husband, wife, spouse
conloco, conlocare, conlocavi, conlocatus	place in order, contract a marriage
conloquium, conloquii, n.	discussion
conquiro, conquirere, conquisivi, conquisitus	hunt, investigate
conscientia, conscientiae, f.	mutual knowledge, complicity
conscriptus, conscripti, m.	senator
*consilium, consilii, n.	council, plan, advice, prudence
consortium, consortii, n.	sharing, partnership
*conspicio, conspicere, conspexi, conspectus	notice, observe, see
constantia, constantiae, f.	constancy
constituo, constituere, constitui, constitutus	decide, establish
*consul, consulis, m	consul
consulatus, consulatus, m	consulship
*consulo, consulere, consului, consultus	consult, consider, advise
consultatio, consultationis, f	full deliberation
consulto, consultare, consultavi, consultatus	deliberate
contentus, contenta, contentum	content, satisfied

continens, continentis, f.	the main point; (here) the mainland
contingo, contingere, contigi, contactus	touch, be associated with
continuus, continua, continuum	uninterrupted
contio, contionis, f.	meeting, assembly
***contra (+ acc.)**	against
contumacia, contumaciae, f.	defiance, perseverance, arrogance, stubbornness
contumax, contumax	proud, insolent
convello, convellere, convelli, convulsus	tug at, pull violently, shake
convicium, convici(i), n.	clamour
convinco, convincere, convici, convictus	overcome, convict of a crime
convivium, convivii, n.	banquet
***copia, copiae, f.**	number, forces, supply (usually plural, but singular in 4.4)
coram (indeclinable)	face-to-face, (as preposition) in the presence of
***corpus, corporis, n.**	body
***corripio, corripere, corripui, correptus**	seize, carry off
corrumpo, corrumpere, corrupi, corruptus	spoil, corrupt, corrupt sexually
creber, crebra, crebrum	crowded, frequent
crebro (indeclinable)	frequently
***credo, credere, credidi, creditus (+ dat.)**	believe, trust, entrust
crimen, criminis, n.	accusation, charge, crime
criminator, criminatoris, m.	accuser
criminor, criminari, criminatus sum	accuse, charge
***crudelis, crudele**	cruel
cubiculum, cubiculi, n.	bedroom
cultus, cultus, m.	honouring, reverence
***cum (indeclinable)**	when, since, although
***cum (+ abl.)**	with
cumulo, cumulare, cumulavi, cumulatus	gather, heap up

cunctatio, cunctationis, f.	delay, hesitation
*cunctus, cuncta, cunctum	all, whole
cupido, cupidinis, f.	desire
*cupidus, cupida, cupidum (+ gen.)	eager (for), greedy
*cupio, cupere, cupivi, cupitus	desire, wish, want
*cur? (indeclinable)	why?
*cura, curae, f.	care, charge, anxiety
curia, curiae, f.	senate house
cursim, (indeclinable)	quickly, cursorily
custos, custodis, m. and f.	guard
damno, damnare, damnavi, damnatus	pass judgement (+ gen. or abl.), find fault with
*de (+ abl.)	about, from, down from
decerno, decernere, decrevi, decretus	decide, decree
*decipio, decipere, decepi, deceptus	deceive
decurro, decurrere, decurri, decursus	run, hasten
dedecus, dedecoris, n.	disgrace, shame
dedico, dedicare, dedicavi, dedicatus	dedicate, consecrate
*defendo, defendere, defendi, defensus	defend
defero, deferre, detuli, delatus	carry down, report
defunctus, defuncti, m.	dead person
dego, degere, degi	pass time
degredior, degredi, degressus sum	march down
dehonesto, dehonestare, dehonestavi, dehonestatus	dishonour, disgrace
*deinde, dein (indeclinable)	then, next, afterwards
deligo, deligere, delegi, delectus	levy, select, enroll
delubrum, delubri, n.	sanctuary
demo, demere, dempsi, demptus	take away
demoveo, demovere, demovi, demotus	dislodge
*denique (indeclinable)	at last, finally, in short
depello, depellere, depuli, depulsus	drive out
deprecor, deprecari, deprecatus sum	pray to be rid of, beg relief from
derigo, derigere, derexi, derectus	direct, set in order
desero, deserere, deserui, desertus	abandon, leave, desert
destinatum, destinati, n.	object, purpose
detestor, detestari, detestatus sum	detest

*deus, dei, m.	god
devotio, devotionis, f.	devotion, sorcery
*dico, dicere, dixi, dictus	say, speak, tell
dictum, dicti, n.	word, order
diduco, diducere, diduxi, diductus	divide, split, deploy
*dies, diei, m, occasionally f.	day
dignatio, dignationis, f.	a deeming worthy, esteem, regard
digno, dignare, dignavi, dignatus	deem worthy
*dignus, digna, dignum (+ abl.)	worthy (of), deserving (of)
diiungo, diiungere, diiunxi, diiunctus	separate
dilectus, dilectus, m.	recruit, conscript
diligo, diligere, dilexi, dilectus	value, single out
*discedo, discedere, discessi	depart, leave
discordia, discordiae, f.	discord
discrimen, discriminis, n.	critical point, dangerous situation
discumbo, discumbere, discubui, discubitus	recline at table
discursus, discursus, m.	a running about, discourse
disertus, diserta, disertum	skilful in speaking
dispergo, dispergere, dispersi, dispersus	scatter about, disperse
dispono, disponere, disposui, dispositus	dispose, station
dissero, disserere, dissui, disertus	examine, discuss
dissimulatio, dissimulationis, f.	dissembling, dissimulation
distraho, distrahere, distraxi, distractus	draw apart, pull apart
*diu (indeclinable)	for a long time
diversus, diversa, diversum	opposite, contradictory
divulgo, divulgare, divulgavi, divulgatus	spread among the people, divulge
*do, dare, dedi, datus	give
*doleo, dolere, dolui	hurt, be in pain, lament
*dolor, doloris, m.	pain, sorrow, anger
*dolus, doli, m.	trick, fraud
dominatio, dominationis, m.	power, dominance
dominor, dominari, dominatus sum	be master, rule over
*dominus, domini, m.	master

*domus, domus, f.	house, home
*donec (indeclinable)	while, until
*donum, doni, n.	gift, present
dubitatio, dubitationis, f.	doubt, wavering judgement
*dubius, dubia, dubium	doubtful, wavering, uncertain
*duco, ducere, duxi, ductus	lead, take, marry, consider
*dum (indeclinable)	while, until, provided that
duodecim (indeclinable)	twelve
*durus, dura, durum	hard, harsh, rough
*e, ex (+ abl.)	from, out of; (in compounds) out
edictum, edicti, n.	edict, proclamation
effero, effere, extuli, elatus	carry out, raise
*efficio, efficere, effeci, effectus	carry out, accomplish
effigies, effigiei, f.	image, likeness, effigy
efflagito, efflagitare, efflagitavi, efflagitatus	demand urgently
effusus, effusa, effusum	flowing, unrestrained, (of persons) prone to
*ego, mei	I, me
*egredior, egredi, egressus sum	go out, come out
egregius, egregia, egregium	extraordinary
elicio, elicere, elicui, elictus	entice, elicit
eloquentia, eloquentiae, f.	eloquence
*enim (indeclinable)	for
enimvero (indeclinable)	and what is more
*eo (indeclinable)	thither
*eo, ire, i(v)i	go
epula, epulae, f.	feast, (pl.) courses of food
epulor, epulari, epulatus sum	feast
*eques, equitis, m.	knight, horseman, (pl.) cavalry
equester, equestris, m.	knight
*equus, equi, m.	horse
erectus, erecta, erectum	upright, bold
*erga (+ acc.)	towards
erigo, erigere, erexi, erectus	raise up, stir up, excite
eripio, eripere, eripui, ereptus	snatch away
*et (indeclinable)	and, both
*etiam (indeclinable)	also, even, still

evinco, evincere, evici, evictus	carry one's point, persuade, overcome
exagito, exagitare, exagitavi, exagitatus	stir up, harass, rouse up
excedo, excedere, excessi, excussus	go beyond, overstep
excelsus, excelsi, m.	noble
excipio, excipere, excepi, exceptus	receive, take, welcome
excrucio, excruciare, excruciavi, excruciatus	torture
excubia, excubiae, f.	watching (pl.)
*exemplum, exempli, n.	example, precedent
exerceo, exercere, exercui, exercitus	drive on, keep busy, discipline
*exercitus, exercitus, m.	army
exin (indeclinable)	after that
exitiosus, exitiosa, exitiosum	pernicious
exitium, exitii, n.	ruin, destruction
exitus, exitus, m.	departure, death
exolesco, exolescere, exolevi, exoletus	grow out of use, stop growing
expedio, expedire, expedi(v)i, expeditus	arrange, set out (an argument or story)
experior, experiri, expertus sum	test, try
expleo, explere, explevi, expletus	complete, fulfil
exprobro, exprobrare, exprobravi, exprobratus	bring up as a reproach
*exspecto, exspectare, exspectavi, exspectatus	wait for, expect
exstimulo, exstimulare, exstimulavi, exstimulatus	stimulate
exter, extera, exterum	outer, extreme, strange
exto, extare, extiti	stand out
*extra (+ acc.)	outside, beyond
extraneus, extranea, extraneum	not of the family
extremu, extremi, n.	limit, outer limit
extrudo, extrudere, extrusi, extrusus	thrust out, force to go out
extruo, extruere, extruxi, extructus	build up
exuo, exuere, exui, exutus	pull off, cast off
fabulosus, fabulosa, fabulosum	storied, fabulous
facies, faciei, f.	appearance
*facilis, facile	easy

*facinus, facinoris, n.	crime, outrage, deed
*facio, facere, feci, factus (in compounds -ficio)	make, do
factum, facti, n.	deed
facultas, facultatis, f.	opportunity, ability, facility
*fallo, fallere, fefelli, falsus	deceive, cheat
falsus, falsa, falsum	wrong, spurious, false
*fama, famae, f.	rumour, fame, glory
familia, familiae, f.	family, household
fastigium, fastigii, n.	summit, pinnacle
fastus, fastus, m.	scorn, contempt
fateor, fateri, fassus sum	confess, disclose
fauces, faucium, f.	throat
faustus, fausta, faustum	favourable, of good omen
fautor, fautoris, m.	patron
*faveo, favere, favi, (+ dat.)	favour, support
favonius, favonii, m.	west wind
favor, favoris, m.	favour, inclination, good-will
fecunditas, fecunditatis, f.	fertility, fecundity, fruitfulness
*femina, feminae, f.	woman
ferme (indeclinable)	nearly, usually, fully
*fero, ferre, tuli, latus	bear, carry, bring, say
*ferox, ferocis (with prefix 'prae-' = very)	fierce, cruel, brave
fessus, fessa, fessum	tired, wearied
*fidelis, fidele	trustworthy, faithful, loyal
fidens, fidens	confident
*fides, fidei, f.	trust, faith, confidence, loyalty
*fido, fidere, fisus sum (+ dat. or abl.)	trust, rely upon
fiducia, fiduciae, f.	trust, confidence
fidus, fida, fidum	faithful
*filia, filiae, f.	daughter
*filius, filii, m.	son
*finis, finis, m.	end, boundary, pl. territory
*fio, fieri, factus sum	become, be made, happen
firmitudo, firmitudinis, f.	stability, firmness
firmo, firmare, firmavi, firmatus	strengthen
flagitiosus, flagitiosa, flagitiosum	disgraceful
flagitium, flagitii, n.	shame, outrage, disgrace

flagito, flagitare, flagitavi, flagitatus	demand urgently
flecto, flectere, flexi, flectus	bend, persuade, prevail upon
fletus, fletus, m.	crying, weeping
floreo, florere, florui, floritus	flourish, bloom, blossom
foedo, foedare, foedavi, foedatus	defile, disgrace
foedus, foeda, foedum	filthy, horrible
foramen, foraminis, n.	hole
forma, formae, f.	form, figure, appearance
formido, formidare, formidavi, formidatus	dread, fear
*forte (indeclinable)	by chance
*fortis, forte	brave, strong, bold
fortuitus, fortuita, fortuitum	casual, accidental, lucky
*fortuna, fortunae, f.	fate, luck, fortune (good or bad)
*forum, fori, n.	forum, market place
foveo, fovere, fovi, fotus	keep warm, favour
*frater, fratris, m.	brother
fraus, fraudis, f.	fraud, deceit
frequens, frequens	crowded, (of persons) assiduous, constant
fretum, freti, n.	strait
*frustra (indeclinable)	in vain
*fuga, fugae, f.	flight, escape
fulgor, fulgoris, m.	brightness, lustre
*fundo, fundere, fudi, fusus	pour, shed, rout
fungor, fungi, functus sum	discharge duty, fulfil
funus, funeris, n.	funeral
gemitus, gemitus, m.	groan
genitus, genita, genitum	begotten
*gens, gentis, f.	race, people, family, tribe, nation
genu, genus, n.	knee
*genus, generis, n.	race, descent, birth, kind
gigno, gignere, genui, genitus	beget; in passive: to be born
gloria, gloriae, f.	glory, renown, praise
gnarus, gnara, gnarum	having knowledge of, aware
*gratia, gratiae, f	favour, thanks, esteem
gratias ago	thank, give thanks
*gravis, grave	heavy, serious, painful, important
*habeo, habere, habui, habitus	have, hold, consider

habilis, habile	handy, apt, fit
*habito, habitare, habitavi, habitatus	live, dwell
habitus, habitus, m.	deportment, appearance, custom
*haud (indeclinable)	not
haurio, haurire, hausi, haustus	drink up, drain, empty
hercule (interjection) (Hercules, Herculis, m.)	by Hercules!
*hic, haec, hoc	this
*hic (indeclinable)	here
*hiems, hiemis, f.	winter, storm
*hinc (indeclinable)	from here, hence, henceforth
honestus, honesta, honestum	distinguished, reputable
*honor, honoris, m.	honour, esteem, glory
horridus, horrida, horridum	frightful, rough
*huc (indeclinable)	here, to this place
*iaceo, iacere, iacui	lie (down)
*iacio, iacere, ieci, iactus (in compounds -icio)	throw
*iam (indeclinable)	now, already
non iam (indeclinable)	no longer
ianitor, ianitoris, m.	door-keeper
Ianuarius, Ianuaria, Ianuarium (mensis)	January (month)
*ibi (indeclinable)	there, then
*idem, eadem, idem	the same
ideo (indeclinable)	therefore, for that reason
idoneus, idonea, idoneum	suitable, convenient
*igitur (indeclinable)	therefore, and so
ignarus, ignara, ignarum	ignorant, unaware
*ignoro ignorare, ignoravi, ignoratus	do not know, be ignorant, misunderstand
ignotus, ignota, ignotum	unknown
*ille, illa, illud	that, he, she, it
*illic (indeclinable)	there
illicio, illicere, illexi, illectus	entice
illuc (indeclinable)	to that place, thither
imago, imaginis, f.	image, statue
imbecillitas, imbecillitatis, f.	weakness
immanis, immane	frightful, monstrous

immensus, immensa, immensum	immense
immineo, imminere	(+ dat.) be a threat to, hang over
immisceo, immiscere, immiscui, immixtus	mix in, unite
impatiens, impatientis	impatient, intolerant (of)
impatientia, impatientiae, f.	impatience, inability to bear (something)
impedio, impedire, impedivi, impeditus	delay, hinder, prevent, hamper
impello, impellere, impuli, impulsus	drive, persuade
impenetrabilis, impenetrabile	impenetrable
***imperator, imperatoris, m.**	emperor, general, leader
imperito, imperitare, imperitavi, imperitatus	rule, command (passive impersonal)
***imperium, imperii, n.**	command, power, empire
***impero, imperare, imperavi, imperatus (+ dat.)**	order, command
impleo, implere, implevi, impletus	fill up, fulfil
implico, implicare, implicavi, implicatus	(of a disease) to take hold
impono, imponere, imposui, impositus	impose, inflict
importuosus, importuosa, importuosum	lacking harbours
impotentia, impotentiae, f.	lack of moderation, uncontrollableness
improvidus, improvida, improvidum	not foreseeing
imprudens, imprudens	incautious, imprudent
impudicitia, impudicitiae, f.	sexual impropriety, adultery, perversity
***in (+ abl.)**	in, on
***in (+ acc.)**	into, onto, against, towards
inanimus, inanima, inanimum	inanimate
inanis, inane	empty, idle, inane
incedo, incedere, incessi, incessus	advance, proceed, cause
***incendo, incendere, incendi, incensus**	burn, set on fire, inflame, rouse
incertus, incerta, incertum	uncertain, inconstant
incido, incidere, incidi, incasus	happen, fall

*incipio, incipere, incepi, inceptus	begin
incoho, incohare, incohavi, incohatus (also 'inchoo')	start, set in motion
incolumis, incolume	unharmed, safe, alive
incolumitas, incolumitatis, f.	safety
inconsultus, inconsulta, inconsultum	rash, unthinking, foolhardy
incredibilis, incredible	incredible, unbelievable
increpo, increpare, increpui, increpitus	rebuke, reprove, reproach
incuso, incusare, incusavi, incusatus	accuse
incurvus, incurva, incurvum	crooked
inde (indeclinable)	from there, thereupon, next
indecorus, indecora, indecorum	unattractive
indicium, indicii, n.	evidence, information
induco, inducere, induxi, inductum	lead in
induo, induere, indui, indutus	put on
ineo, inire, ini(v)i, initus	enter, come into
infaustus, infausta, infaustum	unlucky, ill-omened
infensus, infensa, infensum	hostile
*infero, inferre, intuli, illatus/inlatus	inflict, bring to, cause, carry against
infringo, infringere, infregi, infractus	break off, weaken
*ingenium, ingenii, n.	character, ability
ingredior, ingredi, ingressus sum	enter, undertake
ingruo, ingruere, ingrui	advance threateningly
inhio, inhiare, inhiavi, inhiatus	be avid for, covet
inimicitia, inimicitiae, f.	unfriendliness, hostility, enmity
*inimicus, inimici, m.	(personal) enemy
*iniquus, iniqua, iniquum	unfair, unjust, unfavourable
initium, initii, n.	beginning
inlecebra, inlecebrae, f.	allurement, attraction
inlustris, inlustre	illustrious
inops, inops	weak
*inquam, inquit, inquiunt	say
inrideo, inridere, inrisi, inrisus	laugh at, ridicule
inrogo, inrogare, inrogavi, inrogatus	impose the penalty of
inrumpo, inrumpere, inrupui, inruprus	break in, burst in, assault
insector, insectari, insectatus sum	pursue with hostile intent, dog, victimise

*insidiae, insidiarum, f. pl.	ambush, trap, trick
insido, insidere, insedi, insessus	settle, establish a home
*insignis, insigne	distinguished, glorious
insimulo, insimulare, insimulavi, insimulatus	accuse
insisto, insistere, institi	take a stand, press upon
insociabilis, insociabile	intractable
instans, instans	eager, insisting upon
insto, instare, institi	impend, threaten
insuesco, insuescere, insuevi, insuetus	become accustomed to (+ dat. or abl.)
*insula, insulae, f.	island, block (of apartments)
insulto, insultare, insultavi, insultatus	scoff at, mock
insuper (indeclinable)	above, on top, in addition
intactus, intacta, intactum	untouched
integer, integra, integrum	whole, unbiased, impartial
*intellego, intellegere, intellexi, intellectus	understand, perceive, realise
intendo, intendere, intendi, intentus	stretch out, extend
intentus, intenta, intentum	intent, attentive
*inter (+ acc.)	between, among
*interea, interim (indeclinable)	meanwhile, in the meantime
interdum (indeclinable)	sometimes
interfector, interfectoris, m.	murderer, assassin
internus, interna, internum	internal, domestic
interstinctus, interstincta, interstinctum	spotted, checkered, blotted
intervallum, intervalli, n.	interval, distance
intimus, intima, intimum	most secret, intimate
*intra (+ acc.)	inside, within
introitus, introitus, m.	an entering, a going in
inultus, inulta, inultum	unpunished, unavenged
invidia, invidiae, f.	hatred
*invitus, invita, invitum	unwilling, reluctant
*ipse, ipsa, ipsum	-self
*ira, irae, f.	anger
irrepo, irrepere, irrepsi	creep into
*is, ea, id	this, that, he, she, it
iste, ista, istud	that of yours, such a kind

*ita (indeclinable)	in this way, so, thus
*itaque (indeclinable)	and so, therefore
*iter, itineris, n.	journey, march, way
*iterum (indeclinable)	again
*iubeo, iubere, iussi, iussus	order, command
*iudex, iudicis, m. and f.	judge, juror
iudicium, iudicii, n.	trial, judgement
*iungo, iungere, iunxi, iunctus	join, unite, fasten
iugium, iurgii, n.	quarrel, dispute
ius, iuris, n.	right, duty, justice, one's due
iuveniliter (indeclinable)	youthfully, in an immature way
*iuvenis, iuvenis m. or adj.	young man, young
iuventa, iuventae, f.	the age of youth, youth, state of being young
iuxta (indeclinable)	nearly, equally alike
kalenda, kalendae, f.	first day of the month
labefacio, labefacere, labefeci, labefactum	cause to totter, shake, make fall
*labor, labi, lapsus sum	glide, slip, fall
*labor, laboris, m.	work, toil, trouble
lacrima, lacrimae, f.	tear
*laedo, laedere, laesi, laesus	hurt, injure, harm
laetor, laetari, laetatus sum	rejoice
laquear, laquearis, n.	panelled ceiling
laqueus, laquei, m.	noose, snare
lascivio, lascivire, lascivi, lascivitus	sport, run riot
latebra, latebrae, f.	hiding-place, retreat
*laudo, laudare, laudavi, laudatus	praise
*laus, laudis, f.	praise, honour, credit
*legio, legionis, f.	legion
*lentus, lenta, lentum	slow
levamentum, levamenti, n.	alleviation
levo, levare, levavi, levatus	lift up, ease comfort
*lex, legis, f.	law
*libens, libentis	willing, glad
liberalis, liberale	free, liberal
*liberi, liberorum, m. pl.	children
*libertas, libertatis, f.	freedom
*libertus, liberti, m.	freedman, ex-slave

libido, libidinis, f.	pleasure, desire, lustfulness
*littera, litterae, f. (usually pl. with sg. meaning)	letter
*litus, litoris, n.	sea-shore, beach
*locus, loci, m.	place, position, situation, opportunity
*longus, longa, longum	long
*loquor, loqui, locutus sum	speak, talk
lugeo, lugere, luxi, luctus	mourn, grieve
luxus, luxus, m.	luxury
macto, mactare, mactavi, mactatus	honour, sacrifice
maereo, maerere	grieve, lament
maeror, maeroris, m.	grief
maestitia, maestitiae, f.	sadness
maestus, maesta, maestum	sad
*magister, magistri, m.	teacher, master
magistratus, magistratus, m.	civil office, magistracy
magnitudo, magnitudinis, f.	size, magnitude
*magnus, magna, magnum	big, large, great
*magis (indeclinable)	more, rather
*malo, malle, malui	prefer
*malus, mala, malum	evil, bad
*maneo, manere, mansi	remain, stay
manifestus, manifesta, manifestum	obvious, manifest, plainly guilty, clearly indicating
*manus, manus, f.	hand, band
*mare, maris, n.	sea
maritus, mariti, m.	husband
*mater, matris, f.	mother
materies, materiei, f. (typically only nom. and acc. sing.)	stuff, matter, argument
matertera, materterae, f.	maternal aunt
matrimonium, matrimonii, n.	marriage, matrimony, wedlock
maturo, maturare, maturavi, maturatus	ripen, mature, make haste
medicamen, medicaminis, n.	drug, medicine
medicus, medici, m.	doctor
mediocris, mediocre	average, ordinary
meditor, meditari, meditatus sum	muse over, ponder

memoria, memoriae, f.	memory
memoro, memorare, memoravi, memoratus	remember, recall, remind
*mens, mentis, f.	mind
mereor, mereri, meritus sum	merit, deserve
*metus, metus, m.	fear
*meus, mea, meum	my
*miles, militis, m.	soldier
militaris, militare	military
militia, militiae, f.	military service
mille, in Plural 'milia'	a thousand
minister, ministri, m.	attendant, aide
miraculum, miraculi, n.	a strange thing, a freak occurrence
mirus, mira, mirum	remarkable, strange
misceo, micere, miscui, mixtus	mix, concoct
misericordia, misericordiae, f.	pity, compassion
miseror, miserari, miseratus sum	pity, lament, feel sorry for
mitigo, mitigare, mitigavi, mitigatus	make mild, pacify, soothe, mitigate
mitis, mite	mild
*mitto, mittere, misi, missus (+ prefix 'tra-' = across)	send, throw, let go
modestia, modestiae, f.	discipline
modestus, modesta, modestum	modest, unassuming
modice (indeclinable)	in a restrained manner, modestly
modicus, modica, modicum	moderate, restrained
*modo (indeclinable)	just now, only
*modus, modi, m.	manner, way, kind
*moenia, moenium, n. pl.	city walls, city
moles, molis, f.	massive structure; (here) mole, breakwater
mollio, mollire, moillivi, mollitus	mitigate, make easier, soften
mollis, molle	soft, pliant, tender
*moneo, monere, monui, monitus	warn, advise, teach
monimentum, monimenti, n.	monument, memorial
*mons, montis, m.	mountain
*mora, morae, f.	delay
*morbus, morbi, m.	sickness, disease

*mors, mortis, f..	death
mortalis, mortale	mortal, human
*mos, moris, m	habit, custom, (pl.) character, morals
motus, motus, m.	movement
*moveo, movere, movi, motus	move
*mox (indeclinable)	soon
muliebris, muliebre	of or belonging to a woman, womanly
*multitudo, multitudinis, f.	crowd, multitude
*multus, multa, multum	much, many
municipalis, municipale	provincial (pejorative)
municipium, municipii, n.	town with its own laws, town (generic)
munium, munii, n.	duty
minuo, minuere, minui, minutus	lessen
mutus, muta, mutum	silent
*nam (indeclinable)	for
*narro, narrare, narravi, narratus	tell, relate
*nascor, nasci, natus sum	am born
nativus, nativa, nativum	natural, innate
*natura, naturae, f.	nature
navigium, navigii, n.	ship
*ne (indeclinable)	lest, that not
*nec, neque (indeclinable)	and not, nor, neither
necdum (indeclinable)	and not yet, but not yet
necessitudo, necessitudinis, f.	obligation, intimate bond
*nego, negare, negavi, negatus	say no, deny, refuse, say that . . . not
negotium, negotii, n.	business
*nemo, nullius	no one, nobody
nepos, nepotis, m.	grandson
neptis, neptis, f.	granddaughter
*nescio, nescire, nescivi	not know
nescius, nescia, nescium	unaware, ignorant
nex, necis, f.	death, murder
*nihil (indeclinable)	nothing
nimius, nimia, nimium	too great, excessive
*nisi (indeclinable)	unless, if not, except

nitor, niti, nisus sum	implore, beg on the knees, exert oneself
nobilitas, nobilitatis, f.	nobility
*nolo, nolle, nolui	not want, be unwilling, refuse
*nomen, nominis, n.	name
nominatim (indeclinable)	by name
*non (indeclinable)	not
*nondum (indeclinable)	not yet
*nos, nostrum / nostri	we, us
*noster, nostra, nostrum	our
notesco, notescere, notui	become known, become famous
*notus, nota, notum	known, well-known, famous
*novi, notus (perfect with present meaning)	know
*novus, nova, novum	new, fresh, recent
*nox, noctis, f.	night
nubo, nubere, nupsi, nuptus	marry, be married to
nudus, nuda, nudum	bare, naked
*nullus, nulla, nullum	no, none, not any
*num (indeclinable)	surely . . . not, whether
*numerus, numeri, m.	number
*numquam (indeclinable)	never
*nunc (indeclinable)	now
*nuntio, nuntiare, nuntiavi, nuntiatus	announce, report
*nuntius, nuntii, m.	messenger, message, news
nuptia, nuptiae, f.	marriage, wedding
nurus, nurus, f.	daughter-in-law, wife of grandson/great-grandson
*ob (+ acc.)	because of, on account of
obduco, obducere, obduxi, obductus	draw over as a covering
obeo, obire, obi(v)i, obitus	go to meet
obicio, obicere, obieci, obiectus	throw before, taunt, reproach
obiecto, obiectare, obiectavi, obiectatus	charge, upbraid, reproach
obiectus, obiectus, m.	an opposing, interjection
oblitus, oblita, oblitum	forgetful
obruo, obruere, obrui, obrutus	hide, cover
obscure (indeclinable)	secretly
obscurus, obscura, obscurum	secret, dark, obscure

obtestor, obtestari, obtestatus sum	implore
obverto, obvertere, obverti, obversus	turn towards; (middle sense) turn oneself towards
occasio, occasionis, f.	opportunity, occasion
***octo (indeclinable)**	eight
***occupo, occupare, occupavi, occupatus**	seize, take possession of, occupy
occulto, occultare, occultavi, occultatus	hide, conceal
occultus, occulta, occultum	secret, hidden
occursus, occursus, m	meeting
oculus, oculi, m.	eye
***odium, odii, n.**	hatred
odio est (+ dat.)	be hated by
offensio, offensionis, f.	displeasure, offence
***offero, offerre, obtuli, oblatus**	present, offer
***olim (indeclinable)**	once, formerly, one day
omitto, omittere, omisi, omissus	neglect, disregard, make no mention of
***omnis, omne**	all, every
onero, onerare, oneravi, oneratus	burden, overload; shower with accusations
***onus, oneris, n.**	burden, load
***opera, operae, f.**	work, effort, attention, trouble
opperior, opperiri, opperitus sum	await
oppidanus, oppidani, m. and f.	inhabitant of a town, townsperson
oppono, opponere, opposui, oppositus	oppose, interpose, put oneself in the way
opportunus, opportuna, opportunum	fit, meet, suitable
***opprimo, opprimere, oppressi, oppressus**	overwhelm, crush, weigh down
***ops, opis, f.**	help; (pl.) resources, riches
***opus, operis, n.**	work, toil, construction
***ora, orae, f.**	coast
***oratio, orationis, f.**	speech
orator, oratoris, m.	orator
orbo, orbare, orbavi, orbatus	bereave
ordior, ordiri, orsus sum	begin

*ordo, ordinis, m.	rank, order, line
origo, originis, f.	origin, beginning, lineage
*orior, oriri, ortus sum	rise, start, originate
*orno, ornare, ornavi, ornatus	adorn, decorate, provide, equip
ortus, orta, ortum	born from, descended from
*os, oris, n.	mouth, face
*ostendo, ostendere, ostendi, ostensus	show
ostento, ostentare, ostentavi, ostentatus	show, point out, indicate
*otium, otii, n.	leisure, idleness, peace
paelex, paelicis, f.	mistress, concubine
paeniteo, paenitere, paenitui	give reason for complaint, to feel regret for
*palam (indeclinable)	openly
*par, paris	equal
*parens, parentis, m. and f.	parent; (pl.) relations
paries, parietis, m.	wall
pariter (indeclinable)	equally, together
*paro, parare, paravi, paratus	prepare, provide
*pars, partis, f.	part, some, direction
patefacio, patefacere, patefeci, patefactum	bring to light, reveal
pateo, patere, patui	stand open, be exposed
*pater, patris, m.	father, senator
patientia, patientiae, f.	patience, forebearance
*patior, pati, passus sum	suffer, endure, allow
*patria, patriae, f.	homeland, native land
patro, patrare, patravi, patratus	accomplish
patruus, patrui, m.	uncle (paternal)
*pauci, paucae, pauca	few, a few
*paulatim (indeclinable)	gradually, little by little
paulum, paulo (indeclinable)	a little, somewhat
paveo, pavere, pavi	be frightened of, fear
pavor, pavoris, m.	panic, fear
pectus, pectoris, n.	breast, chest, heart
pelagus, pelagi, m.	sea
pellicio, pellicere, pellexi, pellectus	entice, win over, seduce
*pello, pellere, pepuli, pulsus	push, drive, rout

penas, penatis, m. (typically in plural)	household gods, home (via synecdoche)
penes (+ acc.)	in the power of
***per (+ acc.)**	through, throughout, along
peramoenus, peramoena, peramoenum	very pleasant
percello, percellere, perculi, perculsus	strike down, demoralise
percenseo, percensere, percensui, percensitus	enumerate, examine
percurro, percurrere, percurri, percursus	run through, mention cursorily
***perficio, perficere, perfeci, perfectus**	bring about, complete, perfect
perfugio, perfugere, perfugi	flee
pergo, pergere, perrexi, perrectus	proceed
periculum, periculi, n.	danger
peridoneus, peridonea, peridoneum	very suitable
peritia, peritiae, f.	skill
***peritus perita, peritum (+ gen. or abl.)**	skilled (in)
permisceo, permiscere, permiscui, permixtus	mix thoroughly, involve, embroil
***permitto, permittere, permisi, permissus**	hand over, entrust, permit, allow
permoveo, permovere, permovi, permotus	persuade, prevail upon
pernicies, perniciei, f.	ruin
perodi, perodisse, perosus (perfect tense with present sense)	hate thoroughly
perpetior, perpeti, perpessus sum	endure to the full
perpetro, perpetrare, perpetravi, perpetratus	accomplish
perrumpo, perrumpere, perrupi, perruptus	break through, force a way
pertineo, pertinere, pertinui, pertentus	extend to, affect
***pervenio, pervenire, perveni**	reach, arrive
perverto, pervertere, perverti, perversus	corrupt, overthrow
pervicax, pervicax	determined, steadfast

*peto, petere, petivi, petitus	seek, ask for, make for, attack
pietas, pietatis, f.	piety, loyalty
placeo, placere, placui, placitus	please
*placet, placere, placuit (+ dat.)	it pleases, suits, it is resolved
*plebs, plebis, f.	the people, common people
*plenus, plena, plenum	full, filled
*plerique, pleraeque, pleraque	most, the majority
plerumque (indeclinable)	generally
plus, pluris	more
poculum, poculi, n.	cup, bowl
*poena, poenae, f.	punishment, penalty
pompa, pompae, f.	procession
pomum, pomi, n.	fruit
pone (indeclinable)	(+ acc.) behind
*pono, ponere, posui, positus	put, place, set up (camp)
popularis, populare	popular
*populus, populi, m.	people, nation
*posco, poscere, poposci	demand, ask for
*possum, posse, potui	can, be able
*post (+ acc.)	behind, after
*post (indeclinable)	afterwards, next
*postea (indeclinable)	afterwards, then
posterior, posterius	coming in time after, later
posterus, posteri, m.	descendants (pl.), posterity
*postquam (indeclinable)	after, when
*postremus, postrema, postremum	last
*postulo, postulare, postulavi, postulatus	demand, ask
*potens, potentis	powerful
potentia, potentiae, f.	power
*potestas, potestatis, f.	power, authority, opportunity
potio, potionis, f.	drink, draught
*potior, potiri, potitus sum (+ gen. or abl.)	seize, get possession of
*potius (indeclinable)	rather, more
*praebeo, praebere, praebui, praebitus	provide, give, show, offer
praecello, praecellere	surpass, excel
praecipua, rerum (set phrase)	matters of importance'

praecipuus, praecipua, praecipuum	particular, especial
praeditus, praedita, praeditum	endowed, gifted, possessed of (+ abl.)
*****praemium, praemii, n.**	prize, reward
praefectus, praefecti, m.	Prefect, commander
praefero, praeferre, praetuli, praelatus	carry before, put forward, present
*****praeficio, praeficere, praefeci, praefectus**	put in charge (of)
praegracilis, praegracile	very slender, very thin
praegravis, praegrave	burdensome
praescribo, praescribere, praescipsi, praescriptus	prescribe, use as a pretext
praesens, praesens	present, at hand
praesentia, praesentiae, f.	present time, the present moment
*****praesum, praeesse, praefui (+ dat.)**	be in charge of
praetendo, praetendere, praetendi, praetentus	stretch out, spread, allege
*****praeter (+ acc.)**	beyond, except, besides
*****praeterea (indeclinable)**	besides, moreover, in addition
praetereo, praeterire, praeteri(v)I, praeteritus	pass by, go by
*****praetor, praetoris, m.**	praetor (acted as judge or governor)
praetorius, praetoria, praetorium	of a general; 'Praetorian', i.e. the emperor's bodyguard
praetura, praeturae, f.	praetorship
pravus, prava, pravum	crooked, perverse, depraved
precatio, precationis, f.	prayer, supplication
*****precor, precari, precatus sum**	pray, pray to, beg
premo, premere, pressi, pressus	cover, hold in secret, conceal
prex, precis, f.	prayer, request
*****primus, prima, primum**	first, chief
*****princeps, principis, m.**	emperor, chief, chieftain
principia, principiorum, n. pl.	headquarters
principium, principii, n.	beginning
*****prior, prioris**	previous, former
*****prius (indeclinable)**	before, previously

*priusquam (indeclinable)	before, until
privignus, privigni, m. (privigna, f.)	stepson, (pl.) step-children
*pro (+ abl.)	in front of, for, on behalf of, in return for
probus, proba, probum	(when describing women) virtuous, modest
*procedo, procedere, processi	advance, proceed
proceritas, proceritatis, f.	height
*procul (indeclinable)	far away, distant
*prodo, prodere, prodidi, proditus	produce, betray, surrender
profanus, profana, profanum	profane
profectio, profectionis, f.	a setting out, departure
profero, proferre, protuli, prolatus	bring forward, put off
*proficiscor, proficisci, profectus sum	set out, depart
profundo, profundere, profudi, profusus	pour out
prohibeo, prohibere, prohibui, prohibitus	forbid, prohibit
prolatio, prolationis, f.	postponement, delay
*promitto, promittere, promisi, promissus	promise
promo, promere, prompsi, promptus	bring into view
promptus, prompta, promptum	visible, manifest; (+ infinitive) it is an easy matter to
promunturium, promunturii, n.	promontory
pronepos, pronepotis, m.	great-grandson
pronus, prona, pronum	inclined to, prone, disposed to
propatulus, propatula, propatulum	completely opened
*prope (+ acc.)	near
propero, properare, properavi, properatus	hurry up
properus, propera, properum	quick, hasty
propinquus, propinqua, propinquum	near
proprius, propria, proprium	very own
*propter (+ acc.)	on account of, because of
prorsus (indeclinable)	thoroughly, utterly
prorumpo, prorumpere, prorupi, proruptus	break out, burst out

prospecto, prospectare, prospectavi, prospectatus	gaze out at; (of a place) to look out on
prosperus, prospera, prosperum	agreeable, favourable, fortunate
proveho, provehere, provexi, provectus	advance, carry forward
provenio, provenire, proveni, proventus	come forth, prosper
provideo, providere, providi, provisus	foresee, provide for
*****provincia, provinciae, f.**	province
*****proximus, proxima, proximum**	nearest, next, last
prudentia, prudentiae, f.	prudence, good sense
*****publicus, publica, publicum**	public, common
pudicitia, pudicitiae, f.	chastity, purity
*****pudor, pudoris, m.**	shame, modesty, honour, disgrace
*****pulcher, pulchra, pulchrum**	beautiful, handsome
pulchritudo, pulchritudinis, f.	beauty
*****puto, putare, putavi, putatus**	think, consider, reckon
*****quaero, quaerere, quaesivi, quaesitus**	search for, ask for, ask, inquire
*****qualis? quale**	what sort of?
*****quam, (indeclinable)**	how, than, as
*****quamquam (indeclinable)**	although
quamvis (indeclinable)	however much, although
*****quantus? quanta, quantum**	how big? how much?
*****quasi (indeclinable)**	as if, just as, nearly
-que (indeclinable)	and
*****queror, queri, questus sum**	complain
questus, questus, m.	complaint
*****qui, quae, quod**	who, which, that
*****quia, (indeclinable)**	because
*****quidam, quaedam, quoddam**	one, a certain, some
*****quidem (indeclinable)**	indeed, in fact, however
*****ne ... quidem (indeclinable)**	not ... even
*****quies, quietis, f.**	rest, peace, quiet
quin (indeclinable)	so that not, that not
quinam, quaenam, quodnam	who pray, which pray, what pray?
quippe (indeclinable)	surely, certainly, by all means
*****quis? quid**	who? what? any

*quisquam, quicquam	anyone, anything
*quisque, quaeque, quidque	each, each one, every
*quisquis, quicquid	whoever, whatever
quo, minus (indeclinable)	by which the less; so as to prevent
*quod (indeclinable)	because, (as to) the fact that
quod si	but if
*quomodo? (indeclinable)	how? in what way?
quonam modo (indeclinable)	how
*quoniam (indeclinable)	since
*quoque (indeclinable)	also, too
*rapio, rapere, rapui, raptus	seize, grab, carry off, plunder
raro (indeclinable)	rarely
re- (prefix)	back, again
*recens, recentis	recent, fresh
*recipio, recipere, recepi, receptus	regain, receive, welcome
recludo, recludere, reclusi, reclusus	open up
recondo, recondere, recondidi, reconditus	conceal
*reddo, reddere, reddidi, redditus	give back, restore, hand over, make
*redeo, redire, redii	return, go back, come back
reditus, reditus, m	return
*refero, referre, rettuli, relatus	bring back, report, refer
refuto, refutare, refutavi, refutatus	check, refute
regimen, regiminis, n.	control
*regnum, regni, n.	kingdom, reign, rule
*rego, regere, rexi, rectus	rule, direct
*regredior, regredi, regressus sum	go back, return
*relinquo, relinquere, reliqui, relictus	leave, leave behind, abandon
*reliquus, reliqua, reliquum	the rest of, the other
remedium, remedii, n.	remedy
renideo, renidere	shine, glow, beam with joy
reor, reri, ratus sum	think, reckon
*repente (indeclinable)	suddenly
reperio, reperire, repperi, repertus	discover, learn
repertor, repertoris, m.	discoverer, inventor
*res, rei, f.	thing, affair, matter, business
*res publica, rei publicae, f.	state, republic

resolvo, resolvere, resolvi, resolutus	allow to weaken into indolence (with 'in' + acc.)
responsum, responsi, n.	answer, reply
reticeo, reticere, reticui	keep silent, leave unsaid
*retineo, retinere, retinui, retentus	hold back, restrain, keep
reus, rei, m.	plaintiff, defendant
reviresco, revirescere, revirui	recover
revolvo, revolvere, revolvi, revolutus	(passive, with middle sense) to return to
*rex, regis, m.	king
rima, rimae, f.	chink, crack, cleft
robur, roboris, m.	strength, military strength
*rogo, rogare, rogavi, rogatus	ask, ask for
rostrum, rostri, n.	speaker's platform, Rostrum
rudis, rude	unformed, rough
rumor, rumoris, m.	rumour
rumpo, rumpere, rupi, ruptus	break, burst, break through
rursum (indeclinable)	back, again
rus, ruris, n.	country, countryside
sacer, sacra, sacrum	sacred
sacrifico, sacrificare, sacrificavi, sacrificatus	sacrifice
*saepe (indeclinable)	often
saevio, saevire, saevii, saevitus	be fierce, rage, be mad
saevitia, saevitiae, f.	savagery, cruelty
*saevus, saeva, saevum	savage, cruel
salutatio, salutationis, f.	greeting
*saluto, salutare, salutavi, salutatus	greet, salute
*sanguis, sanguinis, m.	blood
satio, satiare, satiavi, satiatus	satisfy, sate
*satis (indeclinable)	enough
saxum, saxi, n.	rock
*scelus, sceleris, n.	crime, wickedness
*scio, scire, scivi, scitus	know
*scribo, scribere, scripsi, scriptus	write
scriptor, scriptoris, m.	author
*se, sui	himself, herself, itself, themselves
secus (indeclinable)	otherwise, differently
secretum, secreti, n.	secret, private knowledge

secretus, secreta, secretum	secret, hidden, concealed
sectator, sectatoris, m.	follower, devotee
securus, secura, securum	safe, secure
*sed (indeclinable)	but
sedeo, sedere, sedi, sessus	sit
*sedes, sedis, f.	seat, temple, home
segnitia, segnitiae, f.	disinclination for action, sluggishness
*semel (indeclinable)	once
semen, seminis, n.	seed
*semper (indeclinable)	always
*senator, senatoris, m.	senator
senatorius, senatoria, senatorium	senatorial
*senatus, senatus, m.	senate
senecta, senectae, f.	old age
senectus, senectutis, f.	old age
*senex, senis, m.	old man
sepultus, sepulta, sepultum	buried
*sequor, sequi, secutus sum	follow, pursue, attend
series (no gen. or dat.)	succession, sequence
sermo, sermonis, m.	conversation
servitium, servitii, n.	slavery, servitude
*servo, servare, servavi, servatus	save, protect, keep
*servus, servi, m.	slave
set (same as 'sed')	but; yes, and what's more
seu . . . seu (indeclinable)	whether . . . or
severe (indeclinable)	strictly, gravely
severus, severa, severum	stern, severe
sex (indeclinable)	six
*si (indeclinable)	if
*sic (indeclinable)	thus, in this way
sic quoque (indeclinable)	even as it is now
*sicut (indeclinable)	just as, like, as, as if
sidus, sideris, n.	star
*silentium, silentii, n.	silence
simpliciter (indeclinable)	simply, plainly
*simul (indeclinable)	at the same time, together
*simulac (simulatque) (indeclinable)	as soon as
simulatio, simulationis, f.	pretence, deceit

simulo, simulare, simulavi, simulatus	imitate, pretend
***sine (+ abl.)**	without
sino, sinere, sivi, situs	allow, permit
sinus, sinus, m.	anything curved; (here) bay
sisto, sistere, stiti, status	stop, set up, settle
situs, sita, situm	positioned, sited, located
***sive, seu (indeclinable)**	or if, whether
sobrina, sobrinae, f.	second-cousin
socer, soceri, m.	father-in-law
socia, sociae, f.	female companion, partner
societas, societatis, f.	fellowship, complicity
socius, socii, m.	ally, comrade, companion
socors, socors	sluggish, careless
solacium, solacii, n.	comfort, consolation
***soleo, solere, solitus sum**	be accustomed
solitudo, solitudinis, f.	solitude
sollemnis, sollemne	traditional, customary
sollicitudo, sollicitudinis, f.	apprehension
***solus, sola, solum**	alone, only, lonely, single
***somnus, somni, m.**	sleep
sonitus, sonitus, m.	loud noise
sons, sontis (adjective and substantive)	criminal
sordes, sordis, f.	dirt; (pl.) dark clothes worn by mourners, suppliants, or defendants in court
***soror, sororis, f.**	sister
sors, sortis, f.	lot, fate
spado, spadonis, m.	eunuch
spargo, spargere, sparsi, sparsus	divide, distribute, scatter
species, speciei, f.	appearance, pretext, display
***specto, spectare, spectavi, spectatus**	look at, watch
specus, specus, m.	cave, chasm
***sperno, spernere, sprevi, spretus**	despise, reject, scorn
***spero, sperare, speravi, speratus**	hope, expect
***spes, spei, f.**	hope
spiritus, spiritus, m.	breath, life, spirit
sponte (ablative of the assumed noun 'spons')	of one's free will, willingly, voluntarily

*statim (indeclinable)	at once, immediately
*statuo, statuere, statui, statutus	fix, determine, decide, arrange
stimulo, stimulare, stimulavi, stimulatus (+ per = continually)	urge forward, incite
stirps, strirpis, m.	lineage, family, offspring
*sto, stare, steti	stand, stand firm
stringo, stringere, strinxi, strictus (and with prefix 'ad-')	draw, bind, tie to
struo, struere, struxi, structus	construct, contrive
*studium, studii, n.	eagerness, study, devotion
*stultus, stulta, stultum	stupid, foolish
stuprum, stupri, n.	dishonour, illicit sex, sexual outrage, rape
suadeo, suadere, suasi, suasus	recommend, advocate
*sub (+ abl. or + acc.)	under, beneath; up to
subdo, subdere, subdidi, subditus	put under, counterfeit; (perfect passive) suborned
subeo, subire, subi(v)i, subitus	come to, go under
*subito (indeclinable)	suddenly
subnixus, subnixa, subnixum	relying on (+ abl.)
suboles, subolis, f.	shoot, offspring
subsidium, subsidii, n.	help, shelter
subvenio, subvenire, subveni, subventus	come to help, relieve
subverto, subvertere, subverti, subversus	overturn, cause the downfall
successio, successionis, f.	succession
suetus, sueta, suetum	wont, customary
suimet, (genitive 'sui' + -met.)	himself, etc
*sum, esse, fui	be
*summus, summa, summum	highest, greatest, top (of)
*sumo, sumere, sumpsi, sumptus	take, take up
*super (indeclinable)	beyond, besides
superbia, superbiae, f.	arrogance, pridefulness
*superbus, superba, superbum	arrogant
superque, satis ... superque (with partitive genitive)	enough and more than enough of
*supersum, superesse, superfui	be left, remain, survive
suppedito, suppeditare, suppeditavi, suppeditatus	(intransitive) be sufficient, supply the needs

suppleo, supplere, supplevi, suppletus	supply, fill out
supra (indeclinable)	above, beyond
suscipio, suscipere, suscepi, susceptus	take up, undertake, begin, bear
suspendo, suspendere, suspendi, suspensus	suspend, hang, keep poised
suspicio, suspicionis, f.	mistrust, distrust, suspicion
*****suspicor, suspicari, suspicatus sum**	mistrust, suspect
suspirium, suspirii, n.	deep breath, sigh
sustento, sustentare, sustentavi, sustentatus	endure, hold out, maintain
sustineo, sustinere, sustinui, sustentus	support, sustain
*****suus, sua, suum**	his (own), her (own), its (own), their (own)
taceo, tacere, tacui, tacitus	be silent
*****tacitus, tacita, tacitum**	quiet, silent, in silence
taedium, taedi(i), n.	weariness
*****talis, tale**	such
*****tam (indeclinable)**	so
*****tamen (indeclinable)**	however, nevertheless, yet
tamquam (indeclinable)	just as if
*****tandem (indeclinable)**	at last, finally
*****tantum (indeclinable)**	only
*****tantus, tanta, tantum**	so great, such a great, so much
*****tectum, tecti, n.**	roof, house
*****tego, tegere, texi, tectus**	cover, protect, hide
temeritas, temeritatis, f.	recklessness, impetuosity
temperies, temperiei, f.	mixture, temperature
*****templum, templi, n.**	temple
tempto, temptare, temptavi, temptatus	test, try, bribe
*****tempus, temporis, n.**	time
tendo, tendere, tetendi, tensus	stretch out, compete
*****teneo, tenere, tenui, tentus**	hold, keep, maintain
*****terra, terrae, f.**	ground, land, earth
*****terreo, terrere, terrui, territus**	frighten
*****terror, terroris, m.**	terror, panic
testis, testis, m. and f.	witness
theatrum, theatri, n.	theatre
*****timeo, timere, timui**	fear, be afraid

toga, togae, f.	toga
tolero, tolerare, toleravi, toleratus	bear
*tollo, tollere, sustuli, sublatus	raise, lift up, remove, destroy
tormentum, tormenti, n.	rack, torture
torvus, torva, torvum	(of facial expressions) grim
*tot (indeclinable)	so many
totiens (indeclinable)	so often, so many times
*totus, tota, totum	the whole, entire, all
*trado, tradere, tradidi, traditus	hand over, entrust, hand down, surrender
*traho, trahere, traxi, tractus	pull, drag, draw
tranquilitas, tranquilitatis, f.	tranquility
*trans (+ acc.)	across, over
transfundo, transfundere, transfudi, transfusus	decant, transfer, transfuse
trepidus, trepida, trepidum	nervous
tres, tria	three
tribunus, tribuni, m.	tribune
*tristis, triste	sad, gloomy, grim
*tu, tui	you (singular)
*tum (indeclinable)	then, next
tumidus, tumida, tumidum	swollen, bloated
tunc (indeclinable)	then, at that time
*turba, turbae, f.	crowd, mob, disturbance, multitude
turbo, turbare, turbavi, turbatus	confuse, destabilise, disturb
turpis, turpe	shameful, ugly
tutor, tutari, tutatus sum	guard, defend
*tutus, tuta, tutum	safe
*tuus, tua, tuum	your (singular)
*ubi (indeclinable)	where? where, when
*ubique (indeclinable)	everywhere
ulcerosus, ulcerosa, ulcerosum	full of sores, ulcerous
*ullus, ulla, ullum	any
*ultimus, ultima, ultimum	furthest, last, utmost
ultio, ultionis, f.	revenge, vengeance
ultro (indeclinable)	besides; of one's own accord, voluntarily
ultor, ultoris, m.	avenger, revenger

*umquam (indeclinable)	ever
*una (indeclinable)	together
*unda, undae, f.	wave
*unde (indeclinable)	from where, whence
undecim (indeclinable)	eleven
*undique (indeclinable)	from all sides, on all sides
unicus, unica, unicum	sole, only, single (often substantive)
unus, una, unum	one
*urbs, urbis, f.	city, town, Rome
*usque (indeclinable)	all the way, right up to, continuously
*usus, usus, m.	use, experience, practice, familiarity
usui est	it is useful
*ut (indeclinable) (+ indic.)	as, where, when, how
*ut (indeclinable) (+ subjunc.)	that, so that, to
*uter? utra, utrum	which (of two)?
*uterque, utraque, utrumque	each (of two), both
*utrum (indeclinable)	whether
*utor, uti, usus sum (+ abl.)	use, enjoy
*uxor, uxoris, f.	wife
vacuus, vacua, vacuum	empty
vagus, vaga, vagum	wandering, vagrant
valetudo, valetudinis, f.	good health, health, illness
*validus, valida, validum	strong, powerful
vallus, valli, m.	fortification, palisade
vanus, vana, vanum	empty, vain
vastitas, vastitatis, f.	empty place
-ve (indeclinable)	or
*vel (indeclinable)	or, either
*velut (indeclinable)	just as, like, as, as if
veneficium, veneficii, n.	sorcery, poisoning
venenum, veneni, n.	poison
*venio, venire, veni	come
ventito, ventitare, ventitavi, ventitatus	come regularly
*ventus, venti, m.	wind
verbero, verberare, verberavi, verberatus	beat, strike

*verbum, verbi, n.	word
vere (indeclinable)	truly
vergo, vergere	inlcine, decline
*vero (indeclinable)	indeed, in fact, however
vertex, verticis, m.	top of head
*verto, vertere, verti, versus	turn
*verus, vera, verum	true, real
vescor, vesci	eat
*vester, vestra, vestrum	your (pl.)
*vestis, vestis, f.	clothes
veteranus, veterana, veteranum	old, veteran
*veto, vetare, vetui, vetitus	forbid, order . . . not
*vetus, veteris	old
vetustas, vetustatis, f.	old age
*via, viae, f.	street, road, way, path
vicis (as a genitive; nominative does not exist)	exchange, interchange, duty of one person assumed by another
victima, victimae, f.	sacrificial victim
*video, videre, vidi, visus	see
*videor, videri, visus sum	seem, appear, be seen
vigilia, vigiliae, f.	vigil, watchfulness
viginti (indeclinable)	twenty
*villa, villae, f.	country-house, estate, farm
vinclum, vincli, n.	chain
*vinco, vincere, vici, victus	conquer, defeat, win, be victorious
*vir, viri, m.	man, husband
virilis, virile	manly, of a man, of manhood
*virtus, virtutis, f.	courage, virtue
*vis, pl. vires, f.	force, violence; (pl.) strength, forces
viso, visere, visi, visus	look at attentively, scrutinise
visus, visus, m.	look, sight, appearance
*vita, vitae, f.	life
*vito, vitare, vitavi, vitatus	avoid
*vix (indeclinable)	hardly, scarcely, with difficulty
vocabulum, vocabuli, n.	word, name
*voco, vocare, vocavi, vocatus	call, summon, invite, name

*volo, velle, volui	want, wish, be willing, intend
voluntarius, voluntarii, m.	volunteer
voluntas, voluntatis, f.	good-will, will
voluptas, voluptatis, f.	pleasure
voluto, volutare, volutavi, volutatus	think over, talk over
*vos, vestrum / vestri	you (pl.)
votum, voti, n.	vow, prayer
*vox, vocis, f.	voice, shout, word
vulgaris, vulgare	common, shared, public
vulgo (indeclinable)	publicly, commonly
vulgo, vulgare, vulgavi, vulgatus	spread among the people, make common knowledge
vulgus, vulgi, m.	the people, common people
*vultus, vultus, m.	face, expression